Also available from Continuum

The Teaching Assistant's Guide to Autistic Spectrum Disorders

Ann Cartwright and Jill Morgan

continuum

Continuum International Publishing Group
The Tower Building   80 Maiden Lane
11 York Road   Suite 704
London, SE1 7NX   New York, NY 10038

www.continuumbooks.com

© Ann Cartwright and Jill Morgan 2008

Ann Cartw[...] and Jill Morg[...] [...] [...] der the
Copyright, [...]s and Patents Act [...] [...] be identified [...] Authors of
this work.

British Lib[...] [...] Publ[...]tion Data
A catalogue [...]d for this book is [...]le from the Brit[...] Library.

ISBN 0-8264-9812-4 (paperback)
    978-0-8264-9812-0 (paperback)

Library of Congress Cataloging-in-Publication data
Cartwright, Ann, 1954-
    The Teaching assistant's guide to autistic spectrum disorders / Ann
Cartwright and Jill Morgan.
       p. cm.
    ISBN-13: 978-0-8264-9812-0 (pbk.)
    ISBN-10: 0-8264-9812-4 (pbk.)
 1. Teachers' assistants--Great Britain. 2. Autism--Great Britain. I.
Morgan, Jill, 1956– II. Title.
LB2844.1.A8C37 2008
    371.14'1240941

                                2007038286

Typeset by Kenneth Burnley, Wirral, Cheshire
Printed and bound in Great Britain by MPG Books Ltd,
Bodmin, Cornwall

Contents

Appendix   137

Contents

Introduction

This book has been written for Teaching Assistants (TAs) or Learning Support Assistants (LSAs) or, indeed, for anyone needing to learn more about the condition known as autism. Most support staff want to learn more about the specific difficulties or conditions of the pupils with whom they work, whether they work in special schools, or alongside individual pupils with special needs in mainstream classrooms. Many work with children who have some form of autism or Autistic Spectrum Disorders (ASD). This book is written specifically for those of you who wish to increase your understanding of children with ASD so that you can be more effective in taking their learning forward. The book should be viewed as an introduction to ASD, its effects on children and how best to support them. In the Appendix, you will find some suggested reading and websites that give useful and interesting information on ASD.

Some ask if ASD is a modern phenomenon? Why were children not diagnosed as autistic in the past? We will discuss the history surrounding autism, or ASD, in Chapter 1 but it is generally accepted that more children with ASD are being identified, as awareness of the spectrum increases and diagnosis becomes more effective. Children with ASD have always been around. Now they are, for the most part, identified and, ideally, given greater understanding and support.

Terminology

Before we go any further, it would be useful to discuss briefly the terminology surrounding ASD. Early references to ASD simply used the term autism. It is only in recent years that there has been a fuller appreciation of the range or spectrum of difficulties, behaviours and manifestations of autism: hence the term Autistic Spectrum Disorders has come into use. We will use ASD for simplicity. Children diagnosed with ASD can be charted anywhere along the spectrum in terms of intellectual and behavioural impairments.

We use the term 'children with ASD' rather than 'autistic children', although we acknowledge and agree with the point made by Clare Sainsbury, that people do not just happen to have autism; it cannot be separated in any way from who they are. (Clare Sainsbury is a young woman, in her 20s with Asperger Syndrome, and author of *Martian in the Playground* – see the appendix for details.) When referring to children who do not have ASD we shall use the term *neurotypical* rather than 'normal' as the term reminds us that it is generally agreed that ASD has neurological causes.

Your role as a TA

In England and Wales the government uses the umbrella term 'support staff' to include TAs, clerical and administrative staff. The term 'Teaching Assistant' or 'TA' obviously designates support staff who have direct responsibility for pupil learning. In the 2000 Department for Education and Science (DfES) document *Supporting the TA: A good practice guide*, the support that you provide as a TA is broken down into four areas:

1. Support for pupils – meaning all pupils, not just those you have special responsibility for.
2. Support for teachers, as you carry out your assigned tasks.

3. Support for the curriculum, according to the age group you work with and the type of support you provide.
4. Support for the whole school, as you form part of the school team.

This provides a broad picture of what TAs do and how they fit into the structure of the school.

The role of TAs is very comprehensive, providing support to pupils, teachers, the curriculum and the whole school.

That makes you sound like very valuable team members and important cogs in the machinery of the school. And so it should! Class teachers will tell you that effective TAs are worth their weight in gold!

The DfES document uses terms such as 'assist' and 'support'. These are very general terms. The particulars of *your* role are prescribed by your headteacher and/or supervising teacher, and, on a day-to-day basis in the classroom, are dependent on the children you support, their ages and abilities. It is essential that you understand your role within your particular work setting.

Activity

Answer the following questions to help you define your role:

What are my general duties and responsibilities? It might be helpful to write a list of your responsibilities – you may be surprised to see the extent of what you do.

_____

_____

_____

What am I not expected to do as a TA? This would include responsibilities that are permissible for a TA, but are assigned to someone else in the school, or responsibilities your local authority does not allow TAs to take on.

_____

_____

_____

Discuss your answers with your supervising teacher (or teachers) to ensure you are clear about your role. Your job description will also clarify your responsibilities.

Working under supervision

If you support children with ASD in mainstream settings, the teachers you work with may not be well informed about ASD, its various manifestations and most effective teaching strategies. This is a common occurrence and almost inevitable because mainstream classroom teachers are trained in their subject area, or for a particular age group, and cannot be expected to be experts about all the different disabilities. As the TA, you may be – or may become – the class expert on children with ASD. See page 131 for some basic principles about becoming an effective TA and Jill Morgan's book *How to be a Successful Teaching Assistant* which looks specifically at this (see the Appendix for details).

Even if you feel that you are the expert on ASD in your workplace, and even if you feel that your supervising teacher's approach is inappropriate for children with ASD, you must always:

- have the supervising teacher's permission for any changes to children's routines or behaviour management
- seek his or her advice and guidance on any questions or concerns that you have
- communicate regularly about the work that you do with children
- be diplomatic when giving advice or suggestions.

You may be working in a special school supporting children with ASD, or children with a joint diagnosis of ASD and severe (SLD), or profound and multiple learning difficulties (PMLD). In the latter case it is likely that more attention will be given in the Individual Education Plan (IEP) to the other diagnoses such as visual impairment, seizure patterns or mobility, with ASD considered to be a secondary condition. Of course proper attention must be given to other impairments but the autistic tendencies of children can never be dismissed because ASD is pervasive – it is always there. This will become increasingly apparent as you read this book.

> ASD affects everything: the way children perceive the world, the way they think, the way they behave and the way they relate to things and people.

You may have one or more children with ASD in your school or class. If so, you may have already noticed that no two children with ASD are the same. If you look more closely you will see patterns in their behaviour, as the definition of ASD includes impairment in three main areas: communication, social interactions and imagination.

> The particular ways in which the impairments in communication, social interactions and imagination are displayed in individual children may differ substantially.

Through the book we refer mainly to children with ASD. This is because our focus is on TAs and schools. However in the book we also draw on the experiences of adults with ASD: the writings of many of these adults gives us a glimpse of life with ASD and how it affects thinking and behaviour in all situations. We also draw on the writings and research of people, such as Uta Frith and Simon Baron-Cohen, who continue to work towards clarifying our understanding of ASD. This is because, as we have said, understanding of ASD has really only emerged in recent years, and there is still much to be learned.

Regular features

Throughout the book you will find several regular features:

- Key vocabulary is explained in the glossary (see pages 141–4).
- Shaded boxes emphasize new concepts and ideas.
- Stop-and-think opportunities, marked by , remind you to consider the implications of new information on your attitudes to, and work with, children with ASD and their families. Some of these stop-and-think opportunities

ask you about your current views, philosophy or approach.

- Short descriptions or vignettes show the wide variety of manifestations and different characteristics displayed by people with ASD. These have been taken from interviews and personal experiences, as well as from the growing selection of books relating to ASD.
- At the end of each chapter there is an opportunity for you to think about what you have read and learned. This takes the form of a reflective journal entry. Each one has suggestions and questions to prompt your thinking, writing and application of new ideas in the classroom.

The stop-and-think activities and the reflective journal entries can help you to consolidate your learning and to consider new information critically and professionally. No one will check if you have completed these activities and entries, but the process of writing your thoughts on paper encourages you to think more carefully and deeply. Real learning has taken place when we can explain new principles to others or, in this case, to ourselves in the form of written entries. Recording your thoughts and intentions in writing will also help you to remember new information. Take advantage of these opportunities to really increase your understanding.

You may prefer not to write on the book itself – or you may find that you need more space – in which case, keep a separate notebook to record your thinking and reflective journal entries. Under the terms of copyright you can make copies of pages, but *only for your own use*.

We hope you enjoy reading this book. We hope that the information contained in these chapters will:

- make sense of what you have already noticed
- enlighten you further
- inspire you to work with greater understanding and to work more effectively with all children with ASD.

1

What are Autistic Spectrum Disorders?

The purpose of this chapter is to give you a better understanding of Autistic Spectrum Disorders (ASD) and of the wide variety of characteristics that people with ASD may display. We will first look at the historical background, and how various researchers and practitioners have contributed to our understanding of the condition, which includes Asperger Syndrome. We will then consider how common or prevalent ASD is, and look at some of the myths that surround this condition.

Historical background

Eugene Bleuler was a Swiss psychiatrist who introduced the word 'autism' into the English language in 1912. His article in the *American Journal of Insanity* described a characteristic which he found in many patients with schizophrenia: their inability to relate to, and connect with, other people. He coined the term autism, which comes from the Greek word for 'self' (*autos*), because these patients were so caught up in their own world that they were unable to reach out to those around them. However, it was 1943 before autism was recognized as a separate diagnosis or condition. Dr Leo Kanner, an American psychiatrist working in Baltimore, first described 'classic' autism. He emphasized two main characteristics:

- an extreme aloofness from infancy onwards
- an extreme desire for the 'preservation of sameness'.

Kanner's patients were all children, so he referred to their condition as 'early infantile autism.' Kanner described the children as aloof, withdrawn and locked in a world of their own.

> Autism – from the Greek *autos*, meaning 'self', because of the self-centred or inward-focused nature of the disorder.

Lorna Wing and Judith Gould, working in London in the early 1970s, proposed the idea of a Triad of Impairment in relation to ASD. They maintained that children and adults with ASD have impairments in the three areas of:

- communication
- social interaction
- imagination.

This triad is now universally accepted as being typical of children and adults with ASD – this is discussed in greater detail in the next chapter.

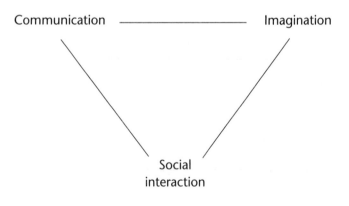

Triad of Impairment

But before we continue, let's briefly consider the term 'impairment'. How would you define impairment?

Activity

Take a moment to write your definition here:

_____

_____

_____

The word impairment suggests a lower level of functioning or a defect in a particular area. For example, people with visual impairments are around us everywhere. You may be one of them. These visual impairments differ in intensity, resulting in differing levels of visual acuity and requiring differing levels of correction with spectacles or contact lenses, but there is still an ability to see. Similarly, we may say that a person is 'hearing impaired' but that simply means a lower level of hearing, rather than complete deafness. Thus although people with ASD have difficulties of some sort when communicating with others, this impairment in communication does not necessarily indicate a total lack of ability to communicate any more than having impaired vision means that a person is blind. Children with ASD may communicate very clearly in all sorts of ways, including some speech, but there will be an impairment or lack of ability compared with what we might expect. This is one of many reminders that this condition occurs across a spectrum – there is always likely to be an impairment, but the degree of severity can vary quite considerably.

Where does Asperger Syndrome fit in?

About the same time that Kanner was developing his ideas about early infantile autism, Hans Asperger, an Austrian doctor working in Vienna, was noticing patterns of behaviour that he labelled 'autistic psychopathy' (literally self-centred personality disease). In 1944, Asperger published his findings about a group of children he described as having 'considerable and very typical difficulties of social integration' and 'particular originality of thought and experience.' The main characteristics of this group were:

- one-sided conversations
- difficulties making friends
- clumsiness
- a lack of empathy or ability to consider other people's needs and views.

Asperger called these children 'little professors' because of their obsessive interest in a particular subject and the apparent need to tell everyone about that subject in great detail. His research papers were written in German, and they were published during the Second World War, but did not become widely known in Britain and the USA until they were translated into English in the 1990s. The children Asperger studied were for the most part bright and able. He predicted that their particular condition and ways of thinking could lead them to great achievements as adults. Named after him, therefore, Asperger Syndrome is the term given to a high-functioning form of autism.

Although Kanner's work was carried out in the 1940s, it is still highly regarded, as almost all of the characteristics he identified as being typical of ASD are still included in a modern diagnosis of the condition. Asperger's research and name continue to be associated with higher-functioning forms of autism; hence those with Asperger Syndrome would be placed on the intellectually more able end of the autistic spectrum. Children with classic or Kanner's autism tend to have learning difficulties in addition to ASD. Children with Asperger's have average or above average intelligence.

Some specialists in this field include a third category of High-Functioning Autism (HFA); however there is no real agreement as to the exact distinctions between HFA and Asperger's.

<--->

Classic or Kanner's autism   Asperger syndrome
                                      High-Functioning Autism

1912 Eugene Bleuler introduced the term 'autism' into the English language to describe a condition he found in some of his patients with schizophrenia.

1943 Leo Kanner identified autism as a separate diagnosis in children, using the term 'early infantile autism'.

1970s Wing and Gould identified the autism Triad of Impairment: communication, imagination and social interaction.

1990s Hans Asperger's work was translated into English. In 1944 he had identified a high-functioning form of autism in young boys.

How common is ASD?

The National Autistic Society (NAS) carried out a survey in 2002 to get a better idea of how many people in the UK have ASD. They estimated that one person in every 250 would be somewhere on the autistic spectrum. In 2001 the Medical Research Council had estimated that about six children in every 1,000 (about one in 170) under the age of 8 would be on the autistic spectrum. More recently the NAS estimated that about one in every 100 children would be on the autistic spectrum. Whichever estimate you use, that translates into well over half a million people in the UK:

10–12 in an average-size secondary school
2–4 in an average-size primary school.

Certainly it is recognized that about four times as many boys as girls are likely to be somewhere on the autistic spectrum. In the 1980s Lorna Wing conducted research that suggested that 15 times as many boys as girls are diagnosed with Asperger's or High-Functioning Autism.

Activity

Take a moment to think of the context in which you work.

How many pupils are in your school? _____

In view of the most recent NAS statistics (one child in every 100 has ASD), about how many of the pupils in your school could have ASD?

_____

How many pupils do you know of in your school who have been diagnosed as having ASD? _____

Are they boys or girls? _____

What about the adults in your school? Could any of the teachers or support staff you work with have ASD? Can someone on the spectrum become a teacher or TA? As you read through this book, and learn about the various symptoms and manifestations of ASD, you may feel that some of your work colleagues come to mind as examples of presenting those sorts of behaviours. Perhaps you even see some of the behaviours in yourself. But remember the 'S' in ASD – autism is now known as a *spectrum* disorder, because it occurs from very low to very high intensity, with some commonalities across the range. Just beyond the end of that spectrum are what we would consider 'normal' behaviours. Any one of us might behave in ways which could be loosely connected to ASD, but we would not be diagnosed as having ASD or being autistic, because those behaviours are not so severe that they limit our ability to function in society.

We may even feel that we have impaired abilities in one of the triad proposed by Lorna Wing and Judith Gould (see page 10) but typically those with ASD have impairments in all three areas. You may wish to visit the Autism Research Centre's (ARC) website (see the Appendix for details) where there is short questionnaire to help adults identify whether they have undiagnosed ASD.

Estimates of the prevalence of ASD

2001 1 in every 170 children (Medical Research Council)
2002 1 in 250 of the population as a whole (National Autistic Society)
2006 1 in every 100 children (National Autistic Society)

But to return to the estimates of prevalence of ASD. Why, you may ask, are there such discrepancies between the estimates? You will have noticed that the estimates suggest that more people have ASD now than in the past. And there is a feeling that ASD is becoming more common. But this is most likely a reflection of increased awareness and knowledge of the condition, rather than an actual increase. This is not a case of an epidemic or the spread of a disease. More children are now being identified as having ASD as methods of diagnosis are being refined, and more professionals and parents are realizing that it is a recognized condition which qualifies for support.

Although Kanner's and Asperger's research were published over 60 years ago, it takes a long time for such findings to have an impact on a practical, everyday level. Typically, when new medical research findings are published, further research is conducted to verify them and establish whether they describe a unique phenomenon or apply more generally to the population. Very slowly, a clearer picture emerges, which eventually leads to changes in diagnosis and treatment, often supported or prompted by legislation. In the case of a condition such as ASD, the process of researching and developing new methods of diagnosis is made more difficult because the symptoms can vary considerably between individuals. As the definition of ASD has changed considerably over the years, those who would now be diagnosed with ASD would not have been included previously, and would not therefore have contributed to the estimated numbers.

You may also have noticed that the estimates of prevalence of ASD sometimes relate to children, and sometimes to the whole population. Again, this is linked to our developing understanding of ASD. Because we are now more aware of ASD, we can at least keep a count of the numbers of these children as records are kept and services provided. But the adults who have ASD and who went undiagnosed in their childhood because of our lack of understanding are very difficult to identify and count. Some of them – particularly those with Asperger's – lead independent lives and therefore do not draw attention to themselves. Others may have co-occurring conditions such as severe learning difficulties that require lifelong support, so the ASD seems to be a secondary condition. In either case, it makes it very difficult to keep track of adults with ASD; according to the NAS, as of 2007, no studies had been conducted into how many

- Well over 500,000 people in the UK have ASD.
- Boys are four times more likely to have ASD than girls.
- 15 times as many boys as girls have been diagnosed with Asperger Syndrome.

adults have ASD. If you are particularly interested in the statistics, there are more details on the website of the NAS and the ARU (see the Appendix for details).

Activity

When you see the term autism or Autistic Spectrum Disorders what comes to mind? What image do you have of people who are autistic? Take a few minutes to jot down your thoughts about how people with autism typically behave, or what their particular characteristics are.

_____

_____

_____

_____

_____

_____

_____

Your impressions of what ASD looks like, or how it manifests itself in a person's behaviour and abilities, may stem from professional experience of working with a child with ASD; it may be based on personal contacts with people with autism or their families; it may be based on books you have read or films you have seen. Even if you have had experience of only one or two individuals with ASD, you will quickly have realized that no two people with ASD are exactly alike. As we have already mentioned, and will discuss in greater detail in the next chapter, both children and adults with ASD typically have impairments in the three main areas of communication, social skills and imagination. However the extent to which they have difficulty in any or all of those areas varies greatly between individuals, and even between any two people with ASD in one family.

So let's look at some of the myths commonly associated with ASD.

Dispelling the myths

Jealousy of a new baby

Children with ASD typically are not diagnosed with a problem until they are at least toddlers. By then, many children have a younger sibling. Until not many years ago, doctors and other professionals often attributed the toddlers' unwillingness to communicate, play and interact, to have terrible tantrums or to be very picky eaters, to jealousy of the new baby. In truth, although sibling rivalry is a commonly accepted phenomenon, it cannot be blamed for these behaviours in children with ASD, as they occur whether there is a new baby in the family or not.

Refrigerator mothers

This myth was prevalent in the 1950s, when professionals felt that the reason some children were unable to show or tolerate affection (such as hugs and close personal contact) was because their cold-hearted mothers had never shown affection to them. In reality, children who have classic Kanner's show little or no interest in other people from their earliest years, and may never seek or be comfortable with physical human contact. Other people are often treated in the same way as objects – they are useful for meeting a variety of needs. Those with Asperger's typically do engage in social relationships. Fortunately, this myth was thrown out many years ago – though not before many mothers were terribly hurt by the label.

Autistic savants

When you think of people with autism, one of the people who may come to mind is the main character in the 1988 film *Rain Man*. Raymond Babbitt, played by Dustin Hoffman, has a large repertoire of unusual behaviours – repetitive speech patterns, the need for strict routines and a very literal interpretation of language. (Remember that scene where he almost gets run over, because as he is walking across the road the sign changes to a red 'Don't walk' and he stops in the middle?) These odd behaviours cause his screen brother Charlie considerable difficulties and frustration. However he also appears to be a brilliant mathematician, calculating with large numbers in only a few seconds – an ability which his brother exploits in the Nevada casinos, to their mutual advantage. Raymond

Myth The behaviour of children with ASD is a result of sibling rivalry.

Truth ASD is a neurological disorder which can occur in children from a wide range of family backgrounds; children show symptoms of ASD whether there are other children in the family or not.

Myth Children with ASD are the product of 'refrigerator mothers' who are unable to give them affection.

Truth The social impairment typical of classic autism often leads the child to reject physical demonstrations of affection and show little interest in other people.

Myth All people with ASD have an incredible ability with maths or painting or music.

Truth Only about one in ten people with ASD would be considered 'savants' (having unusually high ability in a particular area, such as numbers, drawing or memory.)

Babbitt would be known as an 'autistic savant' but this type of giftedness is not typical of people on the autistic spectrum. Fewer than ten per cent of those with ASD possess so-called savantism (or extremely high ability in a particular area). Savantism is not unique to those with ASD. (In fact, Kim Peek, one of the people on whom Dustin Hoffman's character was modelled, does not have ASD, although he does have the phenomenal memory attributed to Raymond Babbitt.)

Daniel Tammet, the subject of the documentary film *Brain Man*, is autistic and would be considered a savant because of his ability with numbers. However, his savantism emerged after a series of childhood seizures. Fortunately Daniel is able to express himself verbally and wrote *Born on a Blue Day* (see the Appendix for details).

Manifestations

The following two case studies give some indication of the different characteristics children with ASD may display.

 Joe is 14. Until he was three he barely spoke, and was therefore referred for speech therapy. He quickly responded to the therapy and soon began to speak in complete sentences, although he continued to struggle in school and spent playtimes wandering alone around the playground. At the age of 8 he was finally diagnosed with Asperger Syndrome and provided with the support of a TA for 20 hours a week. The TA helped him focus on the tasks in hand and reassured him in social situations.

When he left primary school his parents fought for him to attend a secondary school with a language unit. For the first few years Joe spent about half of his time in the unit; now he attends only 25 per cent of the week. The remainder is spent in mainstream classes, with support, where he often gets top marks for maths and English. He chose his own GCSE options and his teachers predict that he will do well. However Joe still cannot be relied upon to cross the road carefully enough to go to the corner shop on his own. His vocabulary is wide though his speech is somewhat stilted.

Lydia is 13. When it was clear that she was not keeping up with others her age, it was decided she should attend the infant Specialist Teaching Facility (STF) in her local primary school. When she moved up to the junior STF it became clear that her unwillingness to join in group work and her outbursts of uncontrollable behaviour made her unsuitable for the group, so she was sent to a special school for pupils with severe learning difficulties. Lydia found the transition very difficult, and her behaviour was very challenging towards pupils and staff. She inflicted wounds on others and on herself, particularly when required to do things she did not want to do. She threw things and kicked holes in the wall.

Lydia was not given a diagnosis of ASD until she was 11, although a retrospective glance over reports written about her give a clear picture of a child with ASD. In addition, Lydia has learning difficulties. Aged 13 she does not speak, read or write, she has no sense of danger and must be supervised at all times. She can walk, run, jump, dress and feed herself, match letters and words, laugh at stories and communicate through PECS (Picture Exchange Communication System, see page 94). Lydia is in a class with a one-to-one staff:pupil ratio. Her school day is full of a variety of activities. Her visual timetable enables her to deal with change. Her outbursts are fewer. She self-harms less.

As you can see, these two children with ASD are quite different, but in fact both are quite typical, and demonstrate the need for the word 'spectrum' when referring to ASD.

Take another look at these two children. What characteristics of ASD do they have in common? Write your thoughts here:

_____

_____

_____

_____

_____

_____

_____

The education, home life and future for these two teenagers are quite different, but both have impairments in the three areas (the triad) first noted by Wing and Gould:

- communication
- imagination
- social interaction.

In the Appendix you will find recommended books and other readings relating to ASD. For example, *Sam and George*, written by Charlotte Moore and named after her two autistic sons, is a fascinating and enlightening book, showing how even two brothers with ASD can have quite different behaviours, abilities and impairments. Contrast their lives with that of Temple Grandin, an American university lecturer with ASD. Her book *Thinking in Pictures* is also highly recommended reading, as is *Martian in the Playground*, Clare Sainsbury's description of what school is like from the perspective of someone with Asperger's. Likewise, in his book *Freaks, Geeks and Asperger Syndrome*, teenager Luke Jackson writes about living with ASD. These writings show us how people (children and adults) with ASD view the world, and how this impacts on their communication, interactions and behaviour – and on their families and peers.

Can it be cured?

ASD is a complex neurological condition. As already mentioned, it was once thought to be caused by poor parenting or family dynamics, but we now know better – ASD has a biological basis. Some people believe that ASD is caused by vaccine damage, in particular by the MMR vaccine. The JABS website (www.jabs.org.uk) details some of the research which is thought to support this theory on the page *Autism – Why?*; you must draw your own conclusions as to whether this may be the case for some children. However, it is undeniable that the symptoms of ASD are also apparent in children and adults who have not had the MMR vaccine.

There is no known cure for ASD, although considerable research has been carried out into identifying genetic markers for the condition, and it does sometimes seem to run in families. One of the difficulties with this claim, of course, is that we have not known about ASD long enough to conduct longitudinal family studies which cover several generations. Although no one in previous generations may have been diagnosed as having ASD, family members can sometimes see – in retrospect – that the so-called 'eccentric' behaviour of a grandfather or other deceased relative may have been due to undiagnosed ASD.

ASD is not life-threatening, except that it can have associated depression (more common in those with Asperger's who are aware of being different and unable to understand the world around them). And of course there may be other complications, such as epilepsy, which compromise the child's health, but the ASD in itself poses no particular threat unless it is accompanied by self-harming.

There are discussions around the use of medication for ASD. Anxiety-reducing drugs in particular can help people cope in what is often a confusing and worrying world for them. Some parents also maintain that a gluten- or casein-free diet can help.

 The bottom line: no single treatment or diet can be prescribed, as symptoms and needs vary so widely.

ASD is a lifelong condition. Children with ASD become teenagers with ASD who in turn become adults with ASD. The condition persists, although changes often take place over time. Unfortunately they are not always for the better. Expectations increase as children grow older, which widens the gap between them and their peers, and makes differences more obvious.

For those diagnosed with Asperger's, the future generally looks brighter. The process can be slow and painful, but as they learn the social skills necessary to function in society, their natural abilities can be put to good use. There are many examples of adults with Asperger's who gain professional qualifications, have gainful employment and live independent lives. Others, like Ros Blackburn (a remarkably clever woman with severe ASD of whom you will hear more later) have learned adequate social skills, but continue to need one-to-one support for practical issues such as road safety, shopping and dressing.

Facts about adults with ASD

- A smaller proportion of adults with ASD marry and have children than is typical in the general population, although there is no real evidence as yet whether such marriages are more or less likely to end in divorce.

- A small proportion of adults with ASD – typically those with Asperger's – are able to work independently, although they often have to take work which is below the level of their qualifications, and consequently with relatively low pay. Far more adults with ASD work in sheltered work-shops.

- The internet offers some work opportunities (such as consulting and teleworking) in an environment well-suited to adults with ASD, as it does not involve direct human interaction, and allows them to communicate in a non-threatening environment and at their own pace. The internet also offers opportunities to 'socialize' without physical proximity, eye contact or appropriate posture. (Is that why so many of us like it as a means of commu-nication?)

- Adults with ASD can find themselves in a very real poverty trap, as they work in low-paid jobs or have to live on benefits if they are unable to work.

For children with ASD the picture is very mixed, and directly related to the level of support each individual receives – which is of course where you feature as a TA. As with any neuro-logical, physical or intellectual condition which you encounter in your pupils, you can provide an environment which:

- minimizes rather than highlights the difficulties caused by the condition
- provides opportunities for learning which are accessible, despite the condition.

The remaining chapters of the book are designed to give you a better understanding of how you can provide this support. Chapters 3 and 4 in particular describe effective behaviour management and teaching strategies you can use to support children with ASD.

Chapter summary

In this chapter we have looked at:

- the historical background to what we now refer to as Autistic Spectrum Disorders (ASD)
- its prevalence in the general population
- the wide variety of ways in which it can manifest itself.

We have also considered some of the misconceptions about ASD and its causes. ASD is a lifelong condition, although its impact may change – for better or worse – over time, according to where the person is on the spectrum, the extent to which he or she can acquire new skills, and of course the extent of the support which is provided. Before we move on to considering the effects of ASD in Chapter 2, take some time to answer the questions opposite, which are designed to help you reflect on what you have read and how it may impact your work and interactions with children or adults with ASD.

Activity

Reflective journal

If you currently work with a child with ASD, complete the first part of this reflective exercise. If you do not, complete the second part.

Supporting a child with ASD

Think of the child with ASD who you are assigned to work with. How would you describe his or her behaviour to someone who had never met them? Write a brief vignette or case study of this individual (using a pseudonym or initials to preserve confidentiality), describing:

- how ASD affects their ability to operate in the classroom and at playtime
- how ASD affects their interactions with other people (both children and adults)
- how ASD affects their communication generally.

_____

_____

_____

_____

_____

_____

_____

_____

_____

_____

If you do not currently work with a child with ASD, in the light of what you have read in this chapter, consider how you think ASD would affect:

▨ a child's ability to operate in a classroom setting and a playtime
▨ how it might affect their interactions with other children and adults
▨ how it might affect their communication generally.

_____

_____

_____

_____

_____

_____

_____

_____

_____

2

Understanding the effects
of Autistic Spectrum Disorders

The purpose of this chapter is to help you understand the effects of ASD. We have already discussed how varied the lives and characteristics of children with ASD can be with their differing levels of impairment. In this chapter we discuss the difficulties shared by children with ASD, caused by common features of the disorder that cross the spectrum. Inevitably, to understand better the difficulties experienced by children with ASD we will make comparisons with children whose development is 'normal'; as we stated in the introduction, 'neurotypical' is a term that is often used for those who would not be considered to be on the spectrum. We are 'neurotypical': our brains function in a typical manner. As a result we experience and perceive things differently from children and adults with ASD.

This is a recurring theme for those with ASD. In her book about her two sons with ASD, Charlotte Moore's experiences lead her to conclude that

When you're autistic, *everything* is experienced differently.

The Triad of Impairment

We referred to the Triad of Impairment in the previous chapter (see page 10). Now we will look at it in greater detail.

Lorna Wing and Judith Gould carried out research on a large group of children in the late 1970s in Camberwell, London. As a psychiatrist, Lorna Wing's interest in autism began when her daughter was diagnosed with the condition in the late 1950s. Wing and Gould's findings led them to conclude that Kanner's and Asperger's children all fitted onto a spectrum of autistic disorders. They concluded that all children with ASD have difficulty or impairment in three main areas and initiated the phrase the Triad of Impairment to denote difficulties in:

- communication
- social interaction
- imagination.

Rita Jordan, Professor of Autism at the University of Birmingham, argues that the Triad would be better labelled as impairments in

- communication
- social development
- flexibility in thinking and behaviour.

As you can see these are essentially the same three areas, but Rita Jordan's terminology suggests that change can happen, that learning can take place. The idea of impairments in these three areas is now generally accepted as being typical of ASD.

In Chapter 1 we asked you to consider how you would define the term 'impairment' (see page 10). You may wish to look back at that section before you read more about the Triad of Impairment here. This is also a good point at which to consider some additional questions about impairment.

Activity

Is impairment the same as disability? If not, how do you think they differ? Do you have impairments? Would you consider them to be disabilities? Write your thoughts here:

_____

_____

_____

_____

As complex beings, we all vary in our abilities in the areas of communication, social interaction or imagination. Some adults – and even young children – are expert communicators or highly sociable animals, while others remain tongue-tied or uncomfortable in social settings all their lives. People you know fit anywhere in between. In each of these areas there is a continuum on which we all belong. Children and adults with ASD have impairments or difficulties in all three of these areas.

The ASD Triad of Impairment:

- communication
- social development and interactions
- imagination, or flexibility in thinking and behaviour.

We will briefly describe the results of Wing and Gould's research in each of the areas of the Triad, and then look more closely at their effects.

Communication

In the area of communication, Wing and Gould's research lead them to group children with ASD in the following ways:

- Some children used speech but without appropriate intonation, producing flat, monotonous speaking patterns.
- Many children were echolalic (echolalia means parroting or echoing the speech of others. Sometimes single words are repeated, other times whole sentences. The echoing may be immediate, or days or weeks later. Accent and intonation are copied perfectly.)
- Most children understood speech even if they did not use it, but took things very literally and with no understanding of irony or sarcasm, or other nuances of language. This aspect of communication impairment also affects the ability to understand humour.

One teacher in a special school reports: 'One of my pupils echoed my phrases – "Tidy up time!" or "Let's see what's happening next?", copying my accent and intonation to perfection. At lunchtime she perfectly parroted our dinner lady.'

 Joe's mother relates an instance when the whole family was watching a funny film, and hooting with laughter. Joe joined in, laughing as much as everyone else. When the laughter subsided, Joe asked, 'Why was that funny?'

Speech or verbal communication

As adults, we use language without considering the complex processes that occur as we take in verbal messages (known as receptive language), or as we speak (known as expressive language). Our use of language includes:

- phonology – the ability to recognize and manipulate speech sounds
- syntax – the ability to handle the rules of grammar
- semantics – the ability to understand and create meaning
- pragmatics – the ability to use language for the purpose of communication.

Activity

Think about this for a moment. Can you break down the process of listening and speaking? List all the separate steps of language processing between someone asking you a simple question, such as 'What's the time?' and you giving them an answer.

_____

_____

_____

_____

_____

We listen and hear sounds. Our auditory memory tells us these represent speech. The brain groups sounds into patterns of words and sentences (phonology) and the meaning of those sentences (semantics) – both the literal meaning (syntax) and the underlying meaning (pragmatics) – enabling us to comprehend.

Should we decide to respond, we choose the words that express our thoughts (semantics) and appropriate sentence structure (syntax); then instructions to the speech muscles are coordinated, enabling us to produce a voice which articulates the right sounds (phonology). Our voice speaks fluently and appropriately (pragmatics), with appropriate inflection (also known as prosody).

In addition, we constantly monitor the effect of our language, listening for a reply and noting the non-verbal responses or body language of the person we are talking to. And so the chain continues. Impairment at any stage of the procedure, either receptive or expressive, impedes our ability to communicate.

Neurotypical children manage, almost miraculously, to acquire the language that is spoken around them. Not only are they able to discriminate the human voice from the many other sounds surrounding them, they can also distinguish speech from coughing or laughing. They develop receptive language before expressive language, and at a very young age:

- at just one month old, babies respond to voices
- at three months they coo in response to pleasant sounds
- at six months they turn to look for new and familiar sounds
- at six months babies can also vocalize for attention
- by twelve months they already have an expressive vocabulary of one or two words.

The age at which children become fluent speakers of their home language, and the rate at which their vocabulary and understanding develop can vary quite significantly, without being a cause for concern. Ann Locke (teacher, speech and language therapist and an associate fellow at the University of Warwick) says that it is not until 7 years of age that all children can be expected to have established all speech sounds. However she maintains that children over the age of 4 whose speech is difficult to understand should receive help, because of the negative impact which poor speech will have on their education.

Language requires us to understand and use 'verbal symbols' in thinking and as a form of communication. Early years teachers use graphics (pictures in storybooks, pictures to stand for letters of the alphabet, pictures to label drawers or containers, etc.) to support children as they learn to read and write the language that they have already learned to speak. In the early stages of learning, child will often talk themselves through a task – consciously using verbal symbols to aid the thinking process. These types of symbolic representations become less necessary as children mature and their language and thinking become more fully developed. For some children with ASD, the reverse may be true.

In her 1995 book *Thinking in Pictures*, Temple Grandin, an American university professor and expert in her field who has High-Functioning Autism (HFA) explains:

'Words are like a second language to me . . . When somebody speaks to me his words are instantly translated into pictures.'

Temple Grandin explains that, unlike most people, her thoughts move from the specific image to generalization and concepts. When someone says the word 'dog,' for example, that immediately conjures up in her mind all the dogs she has ever known. It is as if she has a mental card catalogue of all the dogs she has ever met, complete with pictures, through which her memory flips, in chronological order – and at great speed. There is no generic Great Dane for her, but rather a picture catalogue of specific Great Danes she has known. She reports that interviews with other autistic adults confirm that they also think in this pictorial way, although not necessarily to the extent that she does. This type of process may seem cumbersome, but her brain is able to process her card catalogue of pictures so effectively and quickly that there is no delay in her expressive language as she responds. Temple Grandin's particular skill is very useful in her chosen field as she designs equipment for handling livestock. It enables her to perfectly visualize from every angle a piece of equipment she is designing without building a model – rather like the computer graphics programmes now commonly used for technical drawing.

Difficulties or delay in developing speech and language skills are always of concern, and are often a first indicator of developmental difficulties in young children generally. Children with ASD have a range of difficulties or impairments relating to speech or verbal communication. Some have no speech. Those who do have speech tend to sound different from their peers. Perhaps they use a monotonous tone. Perhaps they sound stilted. Consequently, many are diagnosed with language delay and receive input from a speech and language therapist before the ASD is recognized and identified.

Lynne, the mother of 14-year-old Joe who has Asperger's, describes her experience:

'He was referred to the speech therapist by the health visitor when he was about 3, because he wasn't speaking. He could say the odd word but he wasn't speaking as he should have been.

The speech therapist kept telling me he was having a slow start. She would do all these tests, and say "He's a year behind in this . . . he's a year and a half behind in that". I assumed she knew what she was doing so I didn't question it. Then one day she said to me "I think it's his understanding".

Well I was at my wits end now. I thought, "What does that mean? What do we do?" So I was talking to somebody I work with who has a daughter with special needs, and I said to her "What do you do? Does she see a speech therapist?" She suggested I get Joe referred to the educational psychologist.

So I went back to the school and I said I wanted him referred to the educational psychologist. I spoke to the Special Educational Needs Coordinator (SENCO), and she said "Well we do get funding for extra help for him". But nobody had told us this. We didn't know!

It took about a year and a half for him to be seen by the educational psychologist. She said he had a severe speech and language disorder and she thought he had Asperger's. So he started going to group speech therapy, and he came on in leaps and bounds. But I'd believed them when they said "He's having a slow start", and you want to believe he's going to come on. You want your child to be normal.'

Children with ASD who do have good verbal skills still have difficulty understanding the rules of conversation:

- They are likely to hog a conversation, talking non-stop about a favourite topic.
- They do not understand the idea of turn-taking so they interrupt constantly.
- They may answer questions with monosyllables. Clare Sainsbury says that when asked a question such as 'Do you know what the time is, please?' the only logical answer for a person with ASD is 'Yes'.
- They may laugh too loud and long.
- They take what people say literally.
- They do not understand irony or sarcasm.
- They need more time to process information; if they are asked a question, they may repeat it to help them process it.

Let's think about some of these.

Taking things literally

Many of the ways we express ourselves rely on non-literal expressions and metaphors. Understatement, sarcasm, irony and idioms are common currency in our everyday language.

Look at this list of common idiomatic phrases. What do we mean when we use each of these phrases? And what does each phrase mean literally?

It's raining cats and dogs.

I've got butterflies in my stomach.

He dropped a clanger, didn't he?

Give me a ring later, will you?

She's as bright as a button.

We've had a spot of bother with the car.

Put yourself in my shoes.

Activity

These types of phrases are such a natural part of our language we rarely think about them. Watch out for them in the coming days and weeks, and make a note of the ones you and others around you use. Keep this list as a reminder of the need to use language carefully and more literally around children with ASD if you want to ease communication with and for them.

_____

_____

_____

_____

_____

_____

_____

Hogging the conversation

This is a useful place to consider 'impairment' again. You must know people, not considered to be on the autistic spectrum, who, once they get started in a party or in the pub, go on and on talking about their hobby or current line of work? They do not appear to notice that you haven't been able to get a word in edgeways (nice idiom there) for ages or that you are giving out non-verbal signals (like looking at your watch). They monopolize the conversation, giving all sorts of minute details or facts and statistics. There may be a number of reasons why Mr/Mrs Neurotypical carries on in this way but it has to be concluded that his/her communication and social skills are impaired. Interestingly, it probably is quite acceptable for such people to talk passionately about one topic when they are among fellow enthusiasts, though presumably everyone would chip in now and then with some relevant piece of information.

Tone of voice

Temple Grandin speaks fluently and clearly but in a flat and toneless voice. Like most people with ASD she has difficulty with prosody – the ability to include appropriate rhythm and intonation in her speech. Similarly, Ros Blackburn is an incredibly able communicator with High-Functioning Autism. She can speak fluently for an hour and a half – without notes – about her life with ASD; but she uses a very strident tone with far more emphasis and facial expressions than one would expect in such a situation. This aspect of verbal communication is what is known as para-verbal communication – conveying meaning through intonation and emphasis.

Activity

Take the following sentence, for example: I don't like chocolate. There are different underlying meanings to the sentence according to which word is stressed. See if you can identify the hidden message in each case (the first one has been done).

	Underlying message
I don't like chocolate	. . . but my sister does.
I **don't** like chocolate	_____
I don't **like** chocolate	_____
I don't like **chocolate**	_____

Even a simple four-word sentence like this one can have four distinct meanings according to which of the words we emphasize. With the same four words, we can:

▪ express our own preference as compared with someone else's
▪ refute an accusation
▪ express the extent of our liking for chocolate
▪ compare our liking for chocolate with our liking for something else.

These sorts of distinctions are entirely foreign to the child with ASD, who cannot read the underlying messages – or produce them.

Non-verbal communication

We support our verbal language (our words) with non-verbal, or body language. Non-verbal language (tone of voice, posture, facial expression) gives almost as much information as verbal language for neurotypical people – especially in social interactions. Body language conveys subtle messages – and sometimes not so subtle messages. Studies show that we send out consistent messages by certain stances or movements.

Let's consider a few:

- Fold your arms and/or cross your legs and you're saying: 'I'm defensive'.
- Rest your chin on your hand and look down and you're saying: 'I'm bored'.

Place both hands under the chin with that same look and you're saying: 'I'm really bored' (although of course the message changes quite drastically with the same pose and glances directed towards someone you find physically attractive).

Bored!

■ Lean back in your chair, arms behind your head and you're saying: 'Don't you wish you were as cool as I am?'

Cool!

■ Stand with your hands loosely at your side and you're saying: 'I'm neutral – I'm open to debate or suggestions'.

Children with ASD understand none of these messages. The spoken word is all-important. It totally overrides non-verbal communication. Where there is a conflict of messages between the verbal and non-verbal, the listener/watcher must make up his or her mind between the 'inconsistent messages of emotion', says Wendy Rinaldi, a teacher and speech and language therapist.

Children with ASD only take the verbal message. They have difficulty with pragmatics, or underlying meanings. Also, when they reply they may express themselves in a totally in-appropriate tone. They may sound angry, confrontational, or belligerent although the words may be innocent enough. The tone of voice does not match the message.

Gaze

Appropriate eye contact is an important part of communication for us all. It is one of those non-verbal cues that we all notice – we may feel suspicious of people who will not look us in the eye or threatened by those who glare at us. There is a delicate balance in what are considered appropriate conversational exchanges between making eye contact but not keeping it for too long. Typically, eye contact is difficult for children and adults with ASD. Those able to express themselves say that it is uncomfortable. In addition, the 'soft gaze' – the neutral, non-threatening look considered appropriate and acceptable in our culture during conversation or within a social group, does not come naturally. Instead they may avoid eye contact altogether, or stare and keep eye contact for an overly long time.

If you were asked how long British people typically keep eye contact, you probably would not be able to say. Confronted by someone with ASD, however, you would notice that if they make eye contact, it is likely to be prolonged to an extent that makes you feel uncomfortable – a good indicator that it is not in line with the social norms you have come to expect from your upbringing and experience.

These areas of para-verbal and non-verbal communication are where the distinction between impairment in communication and impairment in social interaction blurs. So much of our social interaction is dependent on our communication skills – and particularly on the subtleties of *how* we say something (verbally and non-verbally) as much as *what* we say. Neurotypical children whose verbal communication is impaired can compensate in some way and be successful in their interactions with others. Children with ASD have difficulties compensating for imperfect verbal communication.

Activity

Think about the children or adults you work with, or know, who have ASD. How would you describe their tone of voice or the way in which they speak?

_____

_____

_____

What about their gaze or look? Do they make eye contact? If they do, how would you describe the way they look at other people? If not, how would you describe their gaze?

_____

_____

_____

Can you describe occasions when they have answered questions or responded to you in a belligerent tone or inappropriate way for no obvious reason?

_____

_____

_____

Social development and interaction

In terms of social interaction, Wing and Gould noted:

■ some children were passive, merely allowing themselves to be hugged or included in a game
■ other children were active but hugged too hard or glared at the other person during these social interactions

- still others, typically the most able group, were over-formal and stilted
- most children were aloof, in a world of their own, giving no eye contact, not even responding to their name.

Let's consider some differences in this area of social development and interaction.

> Joe at age 14 is still quite happy to snuggle up to his mother to watch TV, and happily gives and accepts hugs from his parents.
>
> Sean at age 15 will sit close to his mother, but will not accept hugs.
>
> Lydia at age 13 will sit only on her father's lap at home. In school during trampoline exercises she may sit close to an adult and enjoy firm back patting.

Relationships: do people matter?

Ros Blackburn, who has High-Functioning Autism, maintains that if she kicks an adult who is stopping her doing what she wants to do, it is no different from her kicking the door when it is closed and she wants to get through it. She says we should not take it personally because people do not matter enough to her to hurt them deliberately. You may feel from your own experience that this is not always true. But in general, children with ASD may see no social purpose in relationships – only purposes that benefit them in some practical way.

Let's look at this another way. Consider the different outcomes from 'hurting' a wall and hurting a person. Might the squeals of pain and resentment be more satisfying that the silence of the inanimate wall or door? Past experience may have taught children with ASD (and many neurotypical children) that physical violence does result in a change of environment or attitude, or even get them what they want. Children with ASD like and even need predictability and sameness. Perhaps there is always a predictable outcome when they hit a child or adult. One thing is certain: children with ASD should not be accused of 'attention-seeking' by their behaviours. They may want the reaction or the result but not the attention.

As mentioned, children with ASD often use adults as tools. They may pull an adult by the hand to reach something for them or do something that they cannot, or do not want to do themselves. In these instances they are not actually communicating in any meaningful way in terms of person-to-person relationships. The programme known as PECS (Picture Exchange Communication System) developed in the USA helps children and adults with ASD communicate their needs and wants to others. You will find more about PECS in Chapter 4, where we talk about teaching strategies.

The opinions of others, including parents, teachers and TAs may have little or no influence over the actions of children with ASD. They may do and say exactly what they want, seeming not to care about the outcomes or the feelings of others. They are unable to read the moods of others. This, of course, ties in with their impairment in non-verbal communication but can affect their relationships with their peers. Other children may not want to play with them, finding their behaviours confusing or frightening. Unfortunately some children take advantage of the impairments of the child with ASD by teasing and bullying.

Activity

Stop for a moment and think about children you know who have ASD:

What do they play at playtimes?

_____

Who are their friends?

_____

_____

_____

Do they get teased or bullied?

_____

If yes, when? And why do you think it happens?

_____

_____

_____

Maslow's Hierarchy of Needs

You may have heard the term 'Maslow's Hierarchy' in connection with your work with children. In 1943, the psychologist Abraham Maslow wrote *A Theory of Human Motivation* which proposed that our needs as human beings have a hierarchy or order of priority. This applies to adults as well as children. In order for us to thrive and feel contented and motivated, these needs must be satisfied. Although more than 60 years old, Maslow's theory of a hierarchy of needs remains influential today. He developed this theory by studying people he considered successful or exemplary.

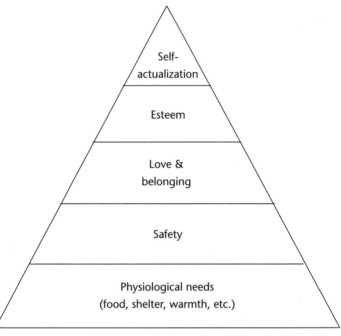

Maslow's Hierarchy of Needs

At the base of the pyramid are the most high priority needs relating to physical comfort, such as food and warmth. Babies operate at this very basic level. But as an adult you know that you can concentrate and cope much better if you are not hungry or getting drenched in the rain. Like babies, we all also thrive better in a safe and caring environment. And so the priority of needs builds, as we seek fulfilment and happiness through a sense of belonging (to family, among peers and in work) and a growing sense of self-esteem as we gain mastery and competence. When all needs are in place then we are ready for 'self-actualization' or the instinctual need we humans have to make the most of our abilities and be the best we can. Where any of these needs remain unfulfilled, it is very difficult for learning to take place and for children or adults to reach their full potential.

Let's look at each of these levels in conjunction with ASD.

Level 1: The need for physical comfort
On the one hand: Children with ASD who are hyposensitive (hypo meaning low) to cold or other physical discomforts, seemingly fulfil this level of need easily.

On the other hand: Hypersensitivity (hyper meaning high) to certain textures and smells can lead to aversions to certain foods, and can make it difficult to ensure an adequate diet.

Level 2: The need to feel safe
On the one hand: Children with ASD may be fearless of physical danger, so they apparently feel safe, or at least do not experience some of the typical fears of childhood.

On the other hand: This exposes them to risk of harm on a daily basis if they cannot, for example, cross the road safely or be left alone in the house. They also can live in an almost permanent state of fear or extreme distress, as we will discuss in greater detail later in the book.

Level 3: The need to belong
On the one hand: A sense of belonging doesn't fit with the autos, self-focus of ASD. Those with ASD typically don't seek the physical contact of loving and caring family relationships.

On the other hand: Authors such as Clare Sainsbury, who has Asperger's, tell us that they feel distinctly 'alien' as if they really do not belong in the society in which they find themselves (hence the title of her book, *Martian in the Playground*).

Level 4: The need for esteem
On the one hand: Typically, children with ASD don't take the opinions of others into account – because they assume that everyone thinks the same way that they do.

On the other hand: Those with Asperger's who are able to communicate their feelings often describe a severe sense of self-doubt as they become aware that they never seem to 'get it right' or understand the rules governing social interactions.

Level 5: Self-actualization

On the one hand: Some individuals with HFA or Asperger's are very successful in their fields of interest or endeavour due to the strengths of ASD – being able to focus on fine detail, having an excellent memory for facts, being totally absorbed by a topic.

On the other hand: ASD is such a pervasive disorder that many children and adults do not acquire the necessary skills to function in our social world.

Many of Maslow's levels of need are linked to social interactions and relationships. Such being the case we may well ask: can children and adults with ASD achieve that state of self-actualization which Maslow saw as the pinnacle of human need?

From what we know of ASD through the personal experiences (usually of people with Asperger's or HFA), the norms that we accept as universal do not necessarily apply to them. When Ros Blackburn was asked if she loved her parents, she replied that she did not know what love meant but that she knew that her parents were people she could trust utterly. The concept of comfort or security for children with ASD must be seen from a different viewpoint. This awareness does not excuse us from trying to meet the needs of children with ASD. Rather it places on us the additional responsibility of looking in a different way to meet the needs of those whose lives are governed by different rules and norms.

Imagination, or flexibility in thinking

Wing and Gould did not say that children with ASD have no imagination; rather that children with ASD cannot imagine the thoughts of others. They noted that the children they studied were all driven by their own intense interests. In addition,

- Some children showed repetitive behaviours such as flapping and spinning, turning lights on and off, wanting family members to always sit in the same seat at meal-times.
- Some were overwhelmed by certain sensory stimuli, and unable to tolerate certain foods, colours or noises.

Sean's mother says that like many teenagers her son dislikes vegetables. But this dislike is based on the texture rather than the taste – he will drink vegetable juice – (parents of neurotypical teenagers, take note!).

- Some showed inappropriate behaviours such as screaming in public and aggression – for no reason that was obvious at the time.
- All were unable to lie.

Joe once said to his Dad, 'You are fat but not as fat as a Sumo wrestler.' Children with ASD cannot lie. They cannot imagine what we want to hear. They tell it as it is. They assume that we think the same as they do.

This last point is particularly interesting, as it links to both communication and social interactions. The child with ASD and well-developed speech, if asked 'Did you like that present?' will almost certainly give you a direct 'Yes' or 'No' – whichever is true. Unless they have been taught otherwise, they will be unable to use the sort of diplomacy that other children learn quite young on receiving an unwelcome gift – 'Thanks, Gran. That's really kind of you' – which does not actually answer the question, but does keep the peace. Nor will they resort to the sarcasm of 'Wow! – just what I really wanted!'.

Ros Blackburn says that she has been taught social graces. She has learned how to reply appropriately and reciprocate when someone says: 'How lovely to see you!'. But she is aware that essentially she is lying because she is *not* pleased to be there chatting with that person. She would rather be somewhere else, engaged in an activity she really enjoys. Andrew Cooksey, a professional consultant who has Asperger's, maintains that the more positive way of describing this inability to lie is to say that children and adults with Asperger's have a keen sense of justice. They see everything as black or white, right and wrong, and so need to speak out when facts and situations are not correctly described.

Routines and predictability

Most of us have our little rituals as we go through the day – checking that we have our keys before we leave the house or lock the car, putting things in cupboards or drawers in a particular way, phoning home or friends, washing hands after using the toilet, etc. When these patterns are disturbed (the mother-in-law never puts the dishes back in the right kitchen cupboard, the mobile rings as we leave the house so we forget to pick up our keys, etc.), we may feel irritated or frustrated, but the effects are usually short-lived. For children with ASD, patterns of behaviour are indispensable, to the extent that they are ritualistic compulsions, causing high levels of anxiety and distress when they are interrupted.

Children and adults with ASD not only *like* things to be predictable, they have a *need* for sameness. As Kanner described it, all of the children he observed had an acute desire for the 'preservation of sameness.' And when that sameness is not preserved, they can suffer acute anxiety and distress.

Imagination

To best describe impairment in this area, Lorna Wing compares young children with ASD with young neurotypical children. Neurotypical children love pretending to be mummy or daddy, doctors and nurses, teachers or firefighters. Initially they copy what they see. Then gradually as they develop they build up imagined conversations and scenarios. Lorna Wing maintains that as we mature, the ability to say 'What if . . . ?' enables you and I to think through possible options and possible effects and results, and so plan our lives. We learn from past experiences and so adjust our ideas.

In contrast, children with ASD lack the ability to say 'What if . . . ?' They do not play imaginary school or spaceman games. They may comb dolly's hair or give a drink to teddy when asked to, but this is not the same as initiating the idea and then taking it further.

As a result, maintains Lorna Wing, even in later years they do not seem able to work out the consequences of their actions. We will return to this point in the next chapter when we discuss behaviour management.

Theory of Mind

In 1985 Simon Baron-Cohen, Alan Leslie and Uta Frith expanded the ASD diagnosis with the Theory of Mind – that is, an ability to understand that other people have thoughts, feelings, and points of view that are not the same as our own. Neurotypical people have the ability to imagine what other people are thinking, or what has motivated them to say or do something.

We see someone running down the road and we think: 'Perhaps they are running for the bus, or perhaps they are late meeting someone.'

We see a smartly dressed couple each wearing a buttonhole and we think: 'Perhaps they are going to a wedding.'

Children with ASD have 'mind-blindness' – they cannot imagine what may be in the mind of another person. People with ASD – children or adults, high IQ or low – have difficulty understanding that your experience of the world is different from theirs. They cannot understand that someone else has a 'mind of their own'. Baron-Cohen, Leslie and Frith illustrated their theory using the 'Sally-Anne Experiment'.

The Sally-Anne Experiment

A group of children, some with ASD, some with Down's syndrome, some neurotypical, were shown two dolls – Sally and Anne – acting out the following:

Sally has a basket.

Anne has a box.

Sally has a marble. She puts the marble in her basket, and leaves the room.

While Sally is away, Anne removes the marble and puts it in her box.

Sally returns.

The children are then asked: 'Where will Sally look for her marble?'

Neurotypical children gave the correct answer – in her basket where she left it. Most of the children with Down's also gave the correct answer.

All but a few of the children with ASD gave the wrong answer. They said Sally would look in the box. They knew the marble was in the box – they had seen Anne put it there when Sally was out of the room. They could not understand why Sally did not know this, *even though they knew Sally had not seen Anne move the marble.*

> Theory of Mind refers to the fact that children with ASD find it very difficult, if not impossible, to imagine the thoughts and feelings of others, or to empathize.

Here is a simple example of how this translates into everyday events:

It's a cold day and you tell the children to put on their coats before going out to play. The child with ASD – because he doesn't feel cold in the classroom – sees no need to wear a coat and makes a big fuss. No matter how much you insist that it is cold and show him that the children who are already outside have their coats on, he will not be able to associate their feelings and actions with his own. He cannot imagine himself in that situation.

There is anecdotal evidence of children and adults with ASD who are in pain or bleeding and who do not ask for help because they assume others know how they feel or what has happened to them. They do not, or cannot, take into account that parents or carers did not see them fall over and hurt themselves, and so do not know that they need help. They do not ask for help because they cannot understand the need to ask in order to get what they need. But Ros Blackburn says if she is hurt or bleeding she does not mention it because she has learned that the result will be close contact, sympathy and – worse still – hugs! This of course relates back to the impairment in social interactions, and the aversion that many children with ASD have to physical contact, or being placed in situations where emotions may be running high – or merely having to interact with other people when they do not understand the ground rules.

Activity

Now that you are aware of the Theory of Mind and the inability of children with ASD to imagine what other people are thinking, how can you better understand the attitudes or behaviour of children you work with who have ASD?

_____

_____

_____

_____

_____

Hyper- and hyposensitivities

Returning to the child who will not put on his coat because he does not feel cold now, it is worth considering that he may not feel the cold when he goes outside. Children with ASD can be hypersensitive to some stimuli and hyposensitive to others. That is, they can have high or low sensitivity to physical stimuli – sound, colour, bodily sensations etc. We will return to this point in Chapter 4, when we discuss how you can help to create an atmosphere that is more conducive to learning for children with ASD by being aware of the effects of external stimuli on their senses.

Coping strategies and comfort zones

Children with autism almost inevitably display bizarre behaviours. Some become obsessive behaviours (such as spinning or flapping). As with all behaviours, they have a purpose. Ros Blackburn says the thing all people with ASD have in common is fear. Children with ASD can live in a state of constant stress or anxiety. Life can be very scary if you cannot make sense of the world around you because of difficulties with communication, empathy or the generalizing of rules and procedures.

Here are some typical obsessive and bizarre behaviour associated with ASD:

- flapping of objects or hands, particularly near the mouth
- flapping dribble
- repeating a behaviour many, many times
- rocking
- attachment to odd objects such as coat hangers, wooden spoons, bits of paper
- repeating phrases or words.

Many of the bizarre or obsessive behaviours in which children with ASD engage are designed to block out stress – or sources of stress. Interestingly most of us display some odd behaviours, some of the time, and to some extent, particularly under stressful conditions. Do any of these sound familiar?

- anxious relatives repeatedly pace hospital corridors waiting for news
- students bite their nails – but only at exam time
- famous sportsmen and women carry 'lucky charms' at important events
- after a shock many people repeat words or phrases over and over
- sensible and intelligent people binge on chocolate or alcohol when stressed or upset
- calm and reasonable people hit out at others when angry or frustrated.

We pace, we binge or we hit out because these actions represent a release of some sort from the stress we are experiencing. They help us cope somehow. The next time you are feeling very stressed, try rocking back and forth for ten minutes. You may be surprised to find quite how calming and pleasant it is. If you persist, it will certainly take up all of your attention and block out external distractions. This is why children with ASD do what they do – it is their version or alternative to having a cigarette or a cup of coffee or a warm bath with the door locked and the radio on full blast.

Here are some other examples of coping mechanisms.

Temple Grandin, an American university professor who specializes in cattle-handling equipment, designed her own 'squeeze machine'. Although she did not want hugs as a child, she realized that being wrapped up tightly was calming and comforting and gave her a sense of well-being. She designed a machine that provided that sense of being held tightly but allowed her to control the level of pressure on her body. She uses her squeeze machine when she is stressed. She uses the same principles in her cattle-handling equipment. Cattle who are to be vaccinated or undergo veterinary procedures – or even those who are being channelled into the abattoir – remain calm and can be handled more humanely if they are contained with just the right amount of pressure.

Sitting in the living room, watching TV, Sean surrounds himself with his books and CDs, making a type of cave. No matter how often his mother gets him to take his stuff back up to his room, it always seem to have sneaked back the next time he's sitting watching TV.

The other all-too-common but rather distressing coping mechanism seen in children with ASD is self-harming. This includes head-banging, scratching or biting often until skin is broken and bleeding. This behaviour also has a purpose. Self-harming has been shown to release endorphins. Endorphins are neurotransmitters that reduce pain and anxiety, enhance the immune system and reduce blood pressure. Self-harming may help children block out distressing or frightening external factors.

What about the family?

Throughout this chapter we have been describing the effects of ASD: that is, we have been describing how the triad can affect the behaviour (in its broadest sense) of children with ASD. We have included a section on relationships, because of the impairment in social interactions, but let's think about relationships a little more.

Most obviously, impairment in social interactions affects the ability of children with ASD to form the sort of meaningful human relationships that we consider to be essential to the well-being of children – affectionate, warm connections which make them feel safe, secure and loved. This will be true of relationships between children and their families and of relationships between children and other adults – and that includes you as a TA.

ASD obviously also has serious implications for family members beyond the direct effects on social interactions and communication. Even children with HFA or Asperger's will impact family dynamics to a significant extent. Family life may be particularly difficult in the early years before diagnosis, but even after special educational provision or support has been put in place family life will never be 'normal.' All children make their mark on a family. Children with ASD have a more complicated impact because of the range of impairments they bring.

School is a form of respite for families where there is a child with ASD, so the child is likely to attend very regularly even if he/she is:

- a little unwell (bowel problems are often an issue for children with ASD so diarrhoea does not necessarily indicate a stomach bug)
- not quite properly or appropriately dressed (maybe those were the only clothes that the parents could get the child to wear that morning)
- smelling a little unhygienic (maybe he refused to change his socks; or brush his teeth or allow anyone else to do it; perhaps she drools or flaps spittle, which quickly produces an unpleasant smell
- covered with bleeding sores (because something unexpected caused him to self-harm and he refuses to let anyone near to clean him up).

Our instinctive reaction to such situations may be something like: 'Why can't these parents take better care of their child?' But remember: if children with ASD live in a state of constant stress, very likely so do their parents – and other family members.

Can you imagine the anxieties of looking after a child who cannot communicate verbally; or who shuns any attempts at affection and treats family with indifference or even apparent hostility; who cannot be left alone or allowed out on his own; and who becomes terribly distressed by something even slightly unfamiliar? If you work with a child with ASD you may already appreciate some of these anxieties, but they must be greatly multiplied for parents and families.

Chapter summary

In this chapter we have given you an overview of the effects of ASD on a child's behaviour and abilities, particularly in the three areas of

- communication
- social skills
- imagination, or flexibility in thinking and behaviour.

You should now have a much clearer understanding of ASD as a pervasive and lifelong condition, affecting all areas of a child's life and functioning.

Activity

Reflective journal

What have I learned in this chapter?

Take some time to reflect on the following questions which relate to the information you have read in this chapter.

1. What changes do I need to make in my outlook or opinions because of what I have read in this chapter?

_____

_____

_____

_____

_____

_____

2. What one thing can I immediately put to use because of what I have read?

_____

_____

_____

_____

_____

_____

_____

Behaviour management and Autistic Spectrum Disorders

Behaviour is a very real and obvious aspect of ASD. You may say that this is true of all children, but children with ASD are generally first noticed because of their behaviours. Some behaviour may be bizarre or disturbing in some way, some may be harmful to the child or others, some may be challenging and difficult to handle. Many books have been written on behaviour management (see the Appendix for details of a book on behaviour management in this series). The purpose of this chapter is to give you a brief overview of the basic principles of managing behaviour. We discuss strategies and techniques that are found to be effective and successful generally. We then consider the extent to which they can be effective for children with Autistic Spectrum Disorders, given the Triad of Impairment, discussed in the previous chapter.

In many ways it is a false distinction to talk of behaviour and learning separately, because everything we do, including learning, could be considered a behaviour. But in this chapter we focus more on what we might term 'social behaviours'. In the next chapter we consider teaching strategies that have been shown to help children with ASD learn; some of these overlap with behaviour management, as they also address more general behaviours.

Some basic principles of behaviour management

The main aim of behaviour management programmes and approaches is to establish and maintain positive and appropriate patterns of behaviour. Too often when we think of behaviour management we automatically think of managing the behaviour of children who disrupt class activities, swear, hit out, or refuse to comply with requests or class rules. We think about managing negative behaviours. In fact *effective* behaviour management is a proactive approach that sets clear expectations for positive and appropriate behaviour, along with the positive consequences that children can expect for compliance. Non-compliance, or misbehaviour, has its own consequences and these must also be made clear, but they should not be the primary focus of a behaviour management approach or plan.

Teachers generally set their expectations for behaviour in the form of class rules. These are usually on display in primary schools, where teachers will also often involve children in deciding class rules, making it more likely that they will remember and comply with them. In secondary school classrooms, rules are less likely to be visibly displayed, or discussed – except in response to offences or non-compliance. Many schools (primary and secondary) ask pupils and their parents to sign contracts indicating that they are aware of the school rules and willing to comply with or support them. Pupils should always be able to answer the questions:

What if I do?
What if I don't?

That is, they should know the consequences of compliance and non-compliance so that they can make a choice between the two. And they need to understand that it is their choice, and that the all too frequent excuse: 'He made me do it!', just won't work. Allowable deviations from the rules should be explored and explained. In general there is a real need for a positive proactive approach rather than a reactive, punitive approach to managing behaviour. Without appropriate behaviour management, classroom activities cannot proceed and learning cannot take place. Effective behaviour management has both social and academic implications.

> The main aim of behaviour management programmes and approaches is to establish and maintain positive and appropriate patterns of behaviour.

For you as a TA, an important issue relating to behaviour management is being aware of your supervising teacher's approach to behaviour and his or her preferred methods of rewarding appropriate behaviour and dealing with inappropriate behaviour. This can vary if you work in more than one class or with more than one teacher. Whatever the context, your approach to behaviour management should always respect the preferences of your supervising teacher. If you support a child with ASD in a secondary school, and move from class to class with that child, you will have to be particularly careful to observe each teacher's preferences.

Some of the children you work with may have an Individual Behaviour Plan (IBP). The IBP is drawn up by the educational psychologist and the teacher. As a TA working one-to-one with the child you may have been invited to contribute to the IBP. An IBP sets out specific strategies for dealing with the behaviours the child typically demonstrates. The advantage of an IBP is that everyone uses the same strategies, so there is a consistent approach.

Activity

Stop for a moment and reflect on the ways in which your supervising teacher manages behaviour. How would you characterize that approach? If you work with more than one teacher, you may want to focus on just one of them. Make a note of some of your thoughts here:

_____

_____

_____

_____

List the rules for the classroom where you work:

1. _____

2. _____

3. _____

4. _____

What rewards does your teacher use for appropriate behaviour?

_____

_____

_____

What sanctions can children expect if they engage in inappropriate behaviour?

_____

_____

_____

Teaching as a behaviour management tool

When we talk about managing behaviour, there are behaviours you would like to see decrease, and behaviours you would like to see increase. Remember that increasing positive behaviour almost always reduces negative behaviour. Inappropriate behaviour is crowded out, as it were, by the appropriate behaviour. Using effective teaching strategies is one of the best behaviour management tools available to you. As children become engaged in the learning process (a positive and appropriate classroom behaviour) they have little time (or inclination) to misbehave. They are motivated by learning. They find the attention and satisfaction they need through successful, positive learning, so the need for inappropriate behaviour decreases.

 You may have noticed too that inappropriate behaviour often comes from less able children. Maybe they cannot complete the task but do not want to admit it, so they deflect attention from their work by 'messing about'. Maybe they are not getting the help they need, so they seek attention through another channel – negative behaviour. Bear this in mind as you find yourself dealing with inappropriate behaviour. When you ask yourself: 'Why is he or she behaving in this way?', the first place to look for an answer is the work that has been set for the child. Is it too difficult? Or is it too easy? Setting work at an appropriate level for a child's abilities and interests is the most effective behaviour management tool available to you.

The ABCs of behaviour

When it comes to modifying inappropriate behaviour, Applied Behaviour Analysis (ABA) is a system which works effectively in situations involving neurotypical children, as well as children with ASD. At its most 'scientific' level it includes a systematic analysis of behaviour which should be carried out by a professional such as a psychologist. The more common version of ABA can be used by anyone who is willing to be consistent and persistent. In fact most schools have a behaviour or discipline policy that takes a behavioural approach, or a cognitive behavioural approach, which also includes discussing behaviour with children. This links back to our initial discussion of rules and consequences, as the procedure relies on an understanding of what have been called the ABCs of behaviour:

A = Antecedent

B = Behaviour

C = Consequence

When a child behaves in a particular way we can look at the *antecedent* – that is, what has come before and prompted or triggered the *behaviour*. And whatever the behaviour, there is always a *consequence* – something will happen as a result of the behaviour. Consequences may be pleasant or unpleasant, depending on whether the behaviour was positive or negative. Take this example of inappropriate behaviour:

Antecedent	Jack pokes Dan in the ribs (just for fun!).
Behaviour	Dan wallops Jack (he doesn't think it's very funny).
Consequence	Jack wallops Dan back.

You know from your own experience that this chain of A > B > C is not going to stop there. The consequence (Jack walloping Dan) will be the trigger for another behaviour – and another consequence:

Antecedent	Jack wallops Dan back.
Behaviour	Dan lets out a yell (he doesn't think being hit is funny either).
Consequence	The teacher or TA intervenes and some sort of warning is given or a sanction is imposed.

As a TA – or a teacher – you would not want to let this sort of behaviour carry on for very long, and you would intervene as soon as possible to put a stop to it.

In the cycle of A > B > C, we cannot always directly change the *behaviour*, but we can affect the behaviour by changing the *antecedent* and/or the *consequence*. We effectively manage behaviour by minimizing possible triggers for negative behaviour and setting up an atmosphere where positive behaviour is rewarded.

Activity

Let's think about some of the possible antecedents for negative behaviour.

If a child hits another child, what might the antecedent or trigger be? Make a note of some possible antecedents in the left-hand column. We'll talk about the right-hand column later.

Behaviour   Emma hits Jade
Possible antecedents: **Can I change this?**

_____   _____

_____   _____

_____   _____

_____   _____

_____   _____

_____   _____

There are plenty of possible antecedents, aren't there? Jade may have been annoying Emma, or may have hit her first, or called her names. Emma may have come into class in a foul mood because of something that happened in the playground or at home before she left for school.

Now let's think about which of these antecedents you could change or remove.

If the behaviour was provoked by:

- another child – you could remove that child, and/or talk to them about their inappropriate behaviour.

- upset over something that happened in the playground – you can watch out for the mood of the children as they enter class and talk to any child who seems to be upset, before he or she is provoked into inappropriate behaviour in class.

Go back to your list of possible antecedents, and fill in the right-hand column according to whether you think you could change or remove them.

No doubt there have been times when you have removed a possible temptation before children notice what mischief they could get up to. Although you probably did not realize it at the time, that was positive – and very effective – behaviour management based on changing the antecedent to inappropriate behaviour. Likewise, you no doubt have used consequences to manage behaviour. Consequences have an interesting double effect. The negative consequences you impose for unacceptable behaviour should discourage a recurrence of the behaviour. Similarly rewards (positive consequences) should increase the recurrence of positive behaviour. These rewards and sanctions then become prompts or antecedents for future behaviour. As children recognize a consistent pattern of:

appropriate behaviour *leads to* **positive consequences**

the positive consequences begin to trigger appropriate behaviour more often – in anticipation of the rewards they have come to expect. Likewise as they see that consistently:

inappropriate behaviour *leads to* **negative consequences**

they become discouraged from behaving inappropriately because they do not want the negative consequence or sanction which they know will be imposed.

You do some of this already, because it feels like common sense. But if you can be more aware of the effects that your deliberate and thoughtful actions can have on children's behaviour, you will be more likely to feel empowered to take action.

Interestingly, we rarely analyse positive behaviour in the same way as negative behaviour. We are so happy to see it occurring, we sigh with relief and rush on to the next task. But it is just as important to look at the ABCs of positive behaviour, because you want it to increase. And you don't have to just hope it will. You can manipulate the antecedents and consequences to increase appropriate behaviour just as much as you can manipulate them to reduce negative behaviour.

> We change **Behaviour** by changing the **Antecedent** and/or the **Consequences**. Manipulating antecedents and consequences increases acceptable behaviours as well as reducing inappropriate behaviours.

How is behaviour linked to the Triad of Impairment?

In Chapter 2 we learned that children with ASD have impairments or difficulties in the three areas of:

- communication
- social interaction
- imagination, or flexibility in thinking and behaviour.

Let's look at each of these areas as they relate to behaviour.

Communication
It has been said that there is no such thing as a naughty child – just a child trying to communicate. Babies cry to communicate. This is not the type of communication we expect in an adult – indeed when we see an adult weeping we know that this must be taken seriously.

But babies cry because that is the only mechanism they possess to communicate their needs. It is not naughty or bad behaviour. Young babies cry because they are non-verbal (or pre-verbal – they have not yet developed speech).

Some children with ASD are non-verbal (and may never develop speech) but they have to have some way to communicate that they need or want something.

 Have you ever been abroad and unable to ask for something simple that you wanted, or more importantly been unable to communicate your feelings or fears? Maybe you were unable to understand what was being communicated to you. Do you remember your frustration? Did you raise your voice or wave your arms, or even stamp a bit? Imagine that frustration as a daily or hourly event and we begin to understand the causes of some modes of inappropriate communication used by children with ASD. Children with ASD will often have what looks like a tantrum. But like all inappropriate behaviour, a tantrum is communication. It tells you that the child is unhappy about something. You have to find out what that something is before you can deal with it. And you usually have to deal with the tantrum first for everyone's sake.

Communication can also be problematic for children with ASD who are verbal. Clare Sainsbury, who has Asperger's, tells in her book of the times when she got into trouble at school for apparently being insolent or sarcastic to a teacher. As we discussed in the last chapter, children with ASD often have a very flat intonation because they have difficulty with prosody (inflection), and this can sound horribly like sarcasm. Many children with ASD also have difficulty processing information. So they may repeat what an adult has said, in an attempt to make sense of it. The combination of flat speech tones and repetition of what someone has just said sounds very much like sarcasm or insolence.

'Look at me when I'm talking to you!' is still an all too frequent refrain in classrooms. We may recognize that eye contact is not considered appropriate in all cultures – for some cultures respect is shown by averting the eyes – but typically we British expect, even demand, eye contact. Children with ASD – some on the severe end of the spectrum who have little or no use for people, and others on the high functioning end of the spectrum with anxiety and frustration as their constant companions – find eye contact unrewarding, challenging or frightening. And when it is made, it may be a blank stare – which again can look like insolence or defiance, even though it is not.

Social interaction

Many people with ASD who can talk about their difficulties describe their life as a condition of almost permanent stress. Clare Sainsbury describes social interaction for children with ASD as 'at best, pointless, at worst, terrifying'. Let's think about the implications of this for a moment. Social interaction happens all the time in classrooms – it is part of the learning process as well as a natural consequence of having many human beings together in a relatively small space. How many times do you think you interact with children or other adults during the day? How many social interactions do children have to have in a normal school day?

Activity

Take a minute to list the necessary social interactions of any child's day.

_____

_____

_____

_____

_____

_____

_____

_____

_____

_____

_____

_____

_____

_____

_____

You will find a list of some we considered essential in the box opposite. In addition there are all those times when children want to interact as part of a natural inclination to socialize. This inclination is typically not present in children with ASD. Children with HFA or Asperger's who may wish to socialize are generally inept because they are unable to understand the rules governing social interactions. However, as you can see from the list it would be difficult for any child to avoid social interaction in the average classroom.

Social interaction – boys playing football

Social interactions which occur during a child's school day	
Asking the teacher questions.	Answering the teacher's questions.
Asking another child for help.	Answering another child's questions.
Asking a teacher/TA for help/equipment.	Asking to go to the toilet.
Answering the register.	Playing team games/sports.
Participating in assemblies.	Reading to an adult.
Taking turns in a game.	Playing at playtime and lunchtime.
Taking a turn to read out loud from a textbook.	Participating in collaborative learning activities.

Let's remember that children with ASD have impairments that range across a whole spectrum, so the ability to communicate varies with each individual. Children with Asperger's often seem to be functioning well in class largely because of their language abilities. And we do tend to judge a person's ability very much by their levels of language, so their inability to interact socially can seem ridiculous or as if they're 'not trying'. As children with ASD get older, the difficulties may increase and become more obvious, because social interactions become more sophisticated. Older children are expected to recognize nuances such as sarcasm and irony in spoken and written language; they are faced with increasingly complex social interactions through their teen years. For children with ASD the primary function of conversation is to impart information; it has no purely social aspect. Social interactions take place purely on a functional level.

Imagination/flexibility
Children with ASD love structure and routines. In fact, they crave routine and structure. Routines and sameness make

sense of their day, eliminate anxiety and reduce inappropriate behaviours such as flapping, self-harming or hitting out at others.

Activity

Think again about a typical classroom. List some of the routines that children face during the course of the school day, term and year.

In the box we have listed some typical school routines. Some apply more to secondary schools and some to primary schools, but an organization such as a school relies on routines for smooth running.

School routines

Registration or form time.

Assembly on certain days of the week.

Bells to signify change of lesson/break/lunchtime/home time.

Movement between classrooms for each subject, or for PE, music or drama, games, etc.

Holidays at Christmas and Easter and in the summer.

Half-term in October, February and June.

Activity

Now think how often we change routines. Routines can change because:

- We decide to be spontaneous and take advantage of a sunny day or a free slot in the computer room.
- An activity takes less or more time than we thought.
- The class is fidgety so we postpone an activity that they may not be able to handle well in that frame of mind.
- There's a fire drill.
- The school photographer is coming that morning.
- A teacher or TA is absent or a child is taken ill.

Peter – a ten year-old with Asperger's – will not even go into school if he knows that his regular TA is absent for any reason. His mother has tried getting around this by not telling him beforehand, but afterwards he was anxious every morning for several weeks in case she was absent again.

Some of these changes in routine are deliberate, others are out of our control. Neurotypical children can cope with these unexpected changes to their routine, but children with ASD cannot, and the result can be distress at best, and violence at worst. It may not be logical for a relatively small hitch in a child's day to result in such disproportionate behaviour, but it is best to accept that it does and to do what you can to prepare the child for changes. Children with ASD need to be helped through even the small regular transitions of the day; in Chapter 4 we will discuss strategies for preparing children for change and transition.

Children with ASD who are well prepared for change and transition will be less anxious or fearful.

Reduction in anxiety or stress = reduction or elimination of inappropriate or unacceptable behaviours.

Can children with ASD control their behaviour?

Children with ASD can be taught to control or change their behaviour through consistent and appropriate behaviour management approaches, and Chapter 4 will discuss some of those which have proven to be most effective. But as we have already stated in this chapter, as adults we need to understand the effects of the child's surroundings and ensure that they are set up so as to prompt appropriate behaviour. Two particular types of situations are the cause of common behavioural difficulties for children with ASD: loosely structured aspects of school life, such as lunchtimes and playtimes, and school field trips.

Unstructured time

Unstructured or loosely-structured times can be particularly difficult for a child with ASD. In school this generally means lunch and playtimes. For neurotypical children this is a time when they can be free from the restraints of the classroom, and socialize freely with their friends. But you already know that children with ASD need structure and routine, and are distinctly uncomfortable in social interactions.

Activity

Think about the school canteen at lunchtime. From what you have already learned about ASD, what aspects of the school canteen can you identify as being potential problems? Make a note of them here and say why you think they would present a problem.

Potential problem: **Because . . .**

_____   _____

                                              _____

                                              _____

_____   _____

                                              _____

                                              _____

_____   _____

                                              _____

                                              _____

_____   _____

                                              _____

                                              _____

For a child who is attached to routines, finds social relationships and physical proximity difficult, is hypersensitive to sounds or smells, and will only tolerate a limited range of foods, the hustle and bustle and the acoustics of the school canteen present enormous difficulties and can result in extreme stress.

A primary school teacher reports:

'In one of the schools where I worked many years ago, we teachers were told that we were losing our free school lunches – much to our indignation – unless we agreed to eat lunch in the school canteen with the children. The free lunch could be then justified on the basis that our presence was a type of supervision. Most teachers took up the offer, but few persisted with it. The horrendous noise spoiled our appetite.'

School trips

School field trips are designed to supplement classroom teaching through a more hands-on, experiential approach to learning. Many children who find it difficult to sit still and concentrate in class do particularly well in this more active learning situation. But for the child with ASD they can be a minefield. Even the short and frequent visits to local places of interest, typical of a special school curriculum, can present significant difficulties.

Take for example a visit to a supermarket to buy ingredients for an upcoming cookery lesson, or for a practical maths activity. Each child will usually have one-to-one support from a teacher, TA or parent; the supermarket visit is focused and relatively brief. But the child with ASD will still often 'misbehave,' perhaps screaming, flapping, hitting out or self-harming; in other words, clearly distressed. What are the triggers for this behaviour? What are the consequences?

Challenging behaviour is very effective because it makes something happen. Lying on the floor in the supermarket generally results in a return to the bus and quiet time with one adult while the rest of the class carries on with the shopping activity. Once the child is removed to the bus, the inappropriate behaviour usually stops. We may say the child is choosing to behave in a particular way as a means to a desirable end –

in this case, getting the exclusive attention of an adult. And this may be true of children in general, but let's not forget what we have already discussed about children with ASD:

- they have considerable difficulty in thinking about the consequences of their actions
- they do not crave attention
- they can easily become overloaded or overwhelmed by external stimuli like noise, lighting or crowds (all present in a typical supermarket)
- screaming or harming self/others releases endorphins which make the child feel better and help block out sensory overload.

Where the neurotypical child may be accused of wanting attention, the child with ASD wants no such thing. But he or she may *need* peace and quiet, and the inappropriate behaviour achieves that end. In this sense, the inappropriate behaviour achieves the desired end, but it is much more likely to be spontaneous than planned or consciously chosen.

ASD: a condition of almost permanent stress

Many people with ASD who can talk about their own experiences describe life with ASD as a condition of almost permanent stress. Here are a few aspects of ASD that cause this stress or anxiety:

- unexpectedly going to art instead of swimming
- sitting in a different place in assembly
- being without your familiar TA because he/she is off sick
- wearing a top that itches
- not knowing why Daddy didn't get you ready for school like he usually does (he's away with work so Mummy did it)
- being unable to take in a situation at a glance and therefore know what is going on (neurotypicals know how to

do that even as quite young children – don't children know when the atmosphere is tense at home and sense there has been an argument while they've been at school?)
- other people's actions which are so illogical to you
- having no idea why everyone else is laughing.

Any one of these factors – and too many others to list – can be a source of considerable frustration and anxiety.

What will motivate appropriate behaviours for the children I work with?

Rewards

A reward is something that reinforces behaviour – that is, it makes it more likely that the behaviour will occur again. The pigeon which pecks on a button and gets food will keep pecking on that button even if food is not delivered every time. The child who gets attention by throwing a tantrum is much more likely to tantrum again when he wants attention. Why change something that works rather than try a more socially-appropriate strategy? Likewise the child who receives positive attention for appropriate behaviour is more likely to behave that way again. So a reward is a motivator. And each of us is motivated by different rewards. Even as adults, we like to be rewarded for our efforts. In fact, we often promise ourselves something rewarding on completion of a task, especially if it is one we dislike:

- When I've put out the bin and washed the kitchen floor, I'm going to sit down with a nice cup of coffee.
- When I've cleaned out the garage, I'll go down the pub.

Neither of these may seem rewarding or motivating to you – or perhaps they both do – but each of us has our preferences and they motivate us. Children with ASD are unlikely to be motivated by the same rewards as other children. You have to find out which toy or activity will motivate the individual child you support. Start by looking at the child's interests or obsessions. Consider the following example:

Lydia, a teenager with ASD and learning difficulties who attends a special school, is particularly fond of straws. She likes to chew and flick them. Lydia has learned that when she completes an activity she can go off and play with a straw for a while. To begin with the straw was placed on the table in front of her. In time the straw-reward did not have to be nearby or visible. It still worked as a motivator.

Sanctions

A punishment or sanction is something that reduces the chance of a particular behaviour occurring again, because it is something the child dislikes. It may be physically uncomfortable, embarrassing or otherwise aversive. However, given the typical preferences of children with ASD, what constitutes punishment for a neurotypical child may have quite the opposite effect for the child with ASD. For example:

- Sending a child with ASD out of the classroom, or away from a group activity may be a pleasure rather than a punishment, if it releases them from unwanted social contact and excessive noise or other stimuli.
- Whereas most children will not enjoy being scolded, children with ASD may feel excited by the shouting adult (face red and eyes bulging) rather than subdued or contrite.
- And remember: sarcasm is not understood by children with ASD.

Sarcasm is never an appropriate form of behaviour management with children but it is completely meaningless in any situation for children with ASD.

Managing your own behaviour

It is uncomfortable to admit it, but sometimes we adults have to change. We have to learn to manage our own behaviour. We are all still learning to be the sort of people we really want to be, so we inevitably make mistakes. But we need to recognize the antecedents for our inappropriate behaviours – especially if we react in a negative way to the inappropriate behaviour of our pupils, rather than being patient and re-teaching what they still need to learn. In the section at the end of the chapter you will find a short self-assessment to help you identify some of the ways in which you may need to change – as well as positive behaviours that you can recognize in yourself.

 Whether you are trying to change your own behaviour or that of one of the children, look for patterns of behaviour or triggers.

Ask yourself: Does this behaviour occur . . .

- at a certain time of day, for example, just before lunch when blood sugars are low and everyone is edgy?
- after a day of rain when there's been no chance to go outside and run around?
- in the presence of a certain person or certain people? (for example, does it occur in a group situation?)
- when the child is asked (or when you are asked) to do a particular thing?
- in a particular place?

Chapter summary

In this chapter we first looked at some basic principles of effective behaviour management, and then considered the extent to which they could be applied to children with ASD. The impairments associated with ASD have a significant effect on behaviour, and also influence the types of rewards and sanctions we can use to manage behaviour. But we can make a difference. We can affect both positive and negative behaviour by changing the antecedents and/or the consequences associated with it. For all children, whether they have ASD or not, rewards and sanctions must be appropriate to the child if they are to be effective. Conforming to acceptable behaviour patterns may be difficult for children with ASD because of impairments in communication, social interaction and imagination. External sensory issues may also result in inappropriate behaviour. Sometimes we adults need to modify our behaviour in order to be more effective classroom managers. At the end of the chapter you will find some questions which will help you reflect on ways you could do this. Many different types of approaches or therapies have been suggested for managing the behaviour of children with ASD. The NAS website includes a great deal of useful information on this topic, as do other sources listed in the Appendix.

In the next chapter we will also discuss a range of effective strategies you can use to help children with ASD better manage their own behaviours.

Reflective Journal

What have I learned in this chapter?

Take some time to reflect on the following questions which relate to the information you have read in this chapter.

1. What changes do I need to make in my outlook or opinions because of what I have read in this chapter?

_____

_____

_____

_____

_____

2. What one thing can I immediately put to use because of what I have read?

_____

_____

_____

_____

_____

3. Look at the list of behaviours below and rate how well you do, by ticking the appropriate column. Remember: being aware is the first step to changing our behaviour!

	Rarely	Always	Only when I'm tired or stressed
Do I . . .			
shout?			
use sarcasm to humiliate children?			
stand over a child until he obeys?			
ridicule a child in front of his friends?			
tut/sigh when a child asks me for help again?			
assume I can make a positive difference?			
challenge a child to do it NOW?			

Choose one of the behaviours from the list that you feel you would like to eliminate, and see what a little determination can do to change your behaviour – as a first step towards being more able to manage the behaviour of your pupils.

	Rarely	Always	Yes, unless I'm tired or stressed
Do I . . .			
acknowledge and reward good behaviour?			
emphasize the carrot more than the stick?			
make sure children understand the consequences of their behaviour?			
individualize rewards to make them motivating?			
maintain a calm and reasonable approach when faced with inappropriate behaviour?			

Give yourself a pat on the back for all the many ways in which you work hard to manage behaviour effectively in the classroom.

4

Teaching children with Autistic Spectrum Disorders

The contributions of adults and children with Asperger's or High-Functioning Autism who can talk and write about their feelings and experiences, help develop strategies for all children with ASD across the spectrum. Clare Sainsbury is one such individual. With a First in philosophy and politics from Oxford University, she also has Asperger's. She is one of many who fulfil Hans Asperger's original prediction that

> 'their narrowness and single-mindedness, as manifested in their special interests . . . can lead to outstanding achievements in their chosen areas'.

Clare Sainsbury's book, *Martian in the Playground*, (see the Appendix for details) is a fascinating – and damning – insight into school life for children and young people with Asperger's. Many of the points raised in the book apply to all children with ASD. Although she was not diagnosed until she was 20, Clare always knew she was different 'in some nameless but all-pervasive way', as she puts it, and by her late teens was severely depressed. No matter how hard she tried she could not be like her peers. As a young child she hoped that one day a spaceship would come and take her away. She felt like an alien put on the wrong planet by mistake. Despite her obvious academic success in school and university, Clare agrees with others with Asperger's who say that school was either terrifying or totally boring. The academic abilities may be different but the impairments are the same. There is much that can, and must, be done to provide a more positive school experience for all children with ASD.

In this chapter, for each of the areas of the triad, we provide some general strategies that are useful to accommodate the impairment, as well as some *Don'ts*. Then for each of the areas we focus on a particular programme or concern:

- the Picture Exchange Communication System (PECS) for communication
- bullying and forming friendships for social interaction
- sensory integration for imagination, or flexibility.

We then describe the TEACCH programme which is commonly used with children with ASD – especially those with learning difficulties. TEACCH addresses the whole Triad of Impairment. And at the end of the chapter we also describe some other programmes that can be used to assist children with ASD in these areas.

Communication

Remember that children with ASD take verbal language very literally, have no understanding of nuance and idioms and do not 'hear' non-verbal communication.

Developing communication

Here are some generally useful suggestions to accommodate impairments in communication:

- Communication should be in clear, simple sentences. A child with ASD may not be able to hold spoken information in his short-term memory long enough to process it and make sense of long strings of information or instructions.
- Avoid giving more than one instruction at a time.
- If the instruction is specifically for the child with ASD, call the child by name first and then give the instruction.

- Avoid repeating an instruction if the child does not respond immediately. Children with ASD may need longer to process language. It does not mean they have not heard nor does it mean that they are being disobedient. Ros Blackburn says that when someone repeats an instruction because she has not responded immediately, she has to begin processing the instruction all over again – word by word.

- Work to the child's strengths and preferred learning style. Some children with ASD do find it easier to process auditory (rather than visually presented) information.

- Use concrete rather than abstract language and learning resources as much as possible.

Here are some *Don'ts* relating to impairments in communication:

- Don't expect children with ASD to be able to generalize. Pieces of information are treated (and mentally filed) separately. They are not assimilated as general principles.

- This also applies to comprehension. Facts may remain separate – the child with ASD may not be able to put them together to make sense of them or build a picture of what is going on. As Clare Sainsbury explains, people with ASD are unable to see the wood for the trees but they do see the individual trees in great detail.

Ros Blackburn talks about a time she did not respond when the red team was told to move somewhere. She responded to her name *Ros*. She did not recognize herself as *the red team*.

How often do you hear yourself saying something like: 'Finish that sentence, and then put your things away in your drawer and go and sit on the mat with the other children'? This type of multiple instruction (this one has five important elements: finish the sentence, put things away, in the drawer, sit on the mat, with other children) is difficult for many neurotypical children to follow, and especially hard for those with ASD.

Picture Exchange Communication System (PECS)

Devised by Lori Frost and Andy Bondy in the USA, PECS is an augmentative communication system designed for children with ASD or other disabilities who have no, or limited, verbal language. PECS augments or adds to children's verbal communication and encourages them to initiate interaction or to ask for something they want by exchanging the picture of an object for the object itself. This system is well-suited to children with ASD because it is consistent, concrete and visual. Briefly, this is how PECS works:

> When a child is first being trained to use PECS, an adult sits across the table from him, offering an object. A picture of that object is on the table between them. The object must be something the child really likes. Food is generally a good motivator, so typically a crisp or a small piece of chocolate is offered. Sitting behind the child is another adult who physically prompts the child to pick up the picture and give it across the table. The food/reward is given immediately in exchange. Another piece is offered and again the child is prompted to exchange the picture for it. At no time does the adult offering the food verbally prompt or encourage the child, because the aim of PECS is for the child to initiate communication.

After the object has been exchanged, the adult will say; 'You wanted a crisp/piece of chocolate' to help establish the connection between the child wanting something and using the picture to get it.As the child learns the system, the physical prompt is no longer used. Gradually the child has to move further away to get the picture.

Teaching PECS

Children can keep their PECS pictures in a book and use them in school, at home or wherever they want as the pictures are easily recognizable. They do not require the expertise required by sign language to present or to understand. Pictures can be quickly and easily produced by using line drawings, digital photography or a very ordinary camera, and can be made-to-measure for each child. Some children may ultimately use PECS to 'say' more complicated things, for example, 'I want a big red ball,' or to express feelings. For more information about PECS, look at the NAS website (see the Appendix for details).

PECS is an excellent system for children with ASD because it is:

- predictable
- structured
- visual
- portable

Activity

If you work with a child with ASD, make a list of objects or activities with which the child is regularly involved.

_____

_____

_____

_____

_____

Tick the items on your list which could be included in a PECS programme (as a drawing or photograph mounted on card) to augment communication for the child.

Social interaction

When we have been born with social intuition, as it has been called, it is difficult to understand what it means to suffer from social blindness. Hans Asperger said of the children he studied that they have to learn everything through the intellect – none of it is intuitive.

Developing social interaction

Here are some useful suggestions relating to impairments in social interactions:

- Accept that children with ASD may speak to you (and the teacher and anyone else) as an equal – the lack of understanding of social hierarchy associated with this impairment can sometimes sound impertinent.
- Teach the child social rules. This is difficult for them – as difficult as you or I may find learning mathematical theorems – but when information is presented as a rule or 'truth' they will find it easier to accept and adopt. The strategy of using social stories – that is, scripts for appropriate social behaviour in a given situation – can be very successful.
- Provide places where children with ASD can enjoy solitude. Playtime is for fun and relaxation. For neurotypical children this typically means the chance to let off steam and make as much noise as they wish with their friends. Fun and relaxation for children with ASD may mean quiet solitude.
- Become familiar with Individual Behaviour Plans (where they exist) so that you do not have to make spontaneous

decisions in reaction to children's inappropriate (or appropriate) behaviour, but can use the agreed-upon strategies. Be *very* consistent in using these strategies.

Here are some *Don'ts* relating to social interaction:

- Don't require children with ASD to participate in group activities any more than is absolutely necessary; group work can be a stressful and an ineffective way of learning for them.
- Don't require them to speak or read out loud, unless you have prepared them for it beforehand and are confident that they are willing and able to do it.
- Don't expect the child to always obey you (or the teacher) without question. If you have said something that is illogical or makes no sense to them, they are likely to challenge or question it.

Bullying

The NAS reported in 2007 that at least 40 per cent of children with ASD are bullied in school, and Clare Sainsbury and others report that being bullied was a routine part of school.

Schools have a clear responsibility to deal effectively with bullying, no matter who is the victim. School policies generally make it clear that verbal insults and taunting are as unacceptable as physical bullying. Check your school's behaviour policy for the section on bullying, and make sure you know what is expected of you as a TA if you discover that a child is being bullied. But consider what you know about children with ASD:

Children with ASD exhibit the sort of characteristics often targeted by bullies:

- bizarre behaviours and obsessions
- atypical tone of voice and unusual (often advanced) vocabulary

- clothes that are not cool
- naïvete and gullibility so they are easily fooled
- literal-mindedness that can be easily exploited
- no tactics for verbal or physical defence.

In addition, children with ASD typically do not tell parents or teachers if they are being bullied, because they assume that the parents and teachers already know, or because they do not understand social norms (i.e. that the bullying should not be happening).

Here are some suggestions for dealing with bullying:

- Put the onus for change on the bully, not the victim: children with ASD are not 'asking to be bullied'.
- Because children with ASD are unable to interpret social signals, they can misinterpret harmless teasing as bullying. You can make this distinction clear for them by explaining: 'When Dan says [give example], he is just teasing. He's not trying to bully you'.
- Don't downplay the effects of the bullying when it really is happening. Telling the child with ASD to 'just ignore it and it will go away' is not helpful – and usually not true.
- Teach children how to react to situations, and be very specific. Telling them what to do when they encounter 'trouble' will not be enough. Describe the situation and what their reaction should be.
- Make sure you do not bully children with ASD yourself – even through expressing mild exasperation when they forget homework, PE kit or library books yet again.

The NAS website has many more practical suggestions for preventing bullying (see the Appendix for details). Of course, all of this should be done under your teacher's supervision and with his or her guidance and approval.

Forming friendships

Children with ASD may not want friends. Those who do – typically children with HFA or Asperger's – have difficulties forming friendships. They may never be invited to parties or to go and play or join a sleepover at another child's house. As with bullying, there are natural tendencies that work against them:

- They often 'tell' on another child who is breaking the rules, due to their fixed belief in rules and fairness and a general anxious belief that rules should be kept.
- They do not always recognize overtures of friendship from other children.
- Their advanced vocabulary and intense interests may lead them to relate more easily to adults than peers.
- Their fixed gaze can be disconcerting.
- Their inappropriate social responses can give them the labels of 'stuck up' or 'rude'.

It is true that some children with ASD may not be looking for friendships and may find it more restful at break time to wander alone around the playground, absorbed in their own inner world. However, there are those who feel alienated and seek to belong, and you can help to facilitate that. The general suggestions we have made for helping social interaction apply here. In addition, perhaps the most helpful thing you can do is explain ASD to other children, so that they can meet children with ASD halfway. Children – particularly in the early years – can be very tolerant, once they understand what is going on.

Imagination/flexibility

Dr Tony Attwood, a clinical psychologist based in Queensland, Australia and an expert on Asperger's, maintains that for children with ASD:

Isolation

the thinking is different, potentially highly original, often misunderstood, but is not defective.

This sense of the way of thinking being different rather than defective is very important. Children with ASD are a minority in our schools but that does not make their way of thinking wrong or worse in some way. It does require the neurotypical majority to stop and think – and act a little differently.

Developing flexibility in thinking and behaviour

Here are some suggestions for strategies that are generally useful in relation to impairments in imagination or flexibility of thinking.

- Obsessive interests can be used to motivate. Temple Grandin's most important mentor in school used her interests to motivate her to do her schoolwork. He did not ridicule her or them.

- Allow children to research their particular interests and strengths, then expand outwards into more general areas and weaknesses.
- Provide appropriate outlets for children to talk about their favourite subjects, rather than trying to suppress or ignore these obsessions.
- Try and pair children with ASD with children who have similar interests or hobbies.
- Set up routines and structure, to create 'sameness' and predictability.

Although these are really important for children with ASD they are unlikely to be able to set them up for *themselves*. If routines have to change, make sure there is ample warning so that children can be prepared for a transition they were not expecting. The TEACCH approach (described later in this chapter) is very useful for this.

- Organize the classroom into discrete areas for activities (with your teacher's approval). Carpets/mats/cupboards /lines on the floor can be used to mark out areas.
- Be more aware of the physical environment of the classroom – the colours, sounds and lighting that are present.
- Help children with ASD to build up their tolerance levels by exposing them to very low levels of stimuli which they find intolerable, and gradually building up their exposure as tolerance levels increase.
- Be prepared to hear some 'truths' you may not like. Children with ASD are unable to understand why they must do things they see as boring, pointless or stupid – and they are very likely to tell you so!

Activity

Stop and think for a moment about the classroom where you work. How would you describe it as a physical environment? Think of the colours, the typical sounds, the lighting, the temperature, the space. Write a brief description here:

_____

_____

_____

When you have a moment, sit in the classroom while all of the children are there, close your eyes and take note of the sounds you can hear. Make a note here of any you missed in your previous description of the classroom.

_____

_____

_____

_____

_____

And while you are sitting there – with your eyes still closed – think about how it feels. Is it too hot/cold? A bit stuffy? Can you sense a lot of movement? Make a note of anything you notice about the feel of the room?

_____

_____

_____

_____

_____

In your description of the classroom, did you use words or phrases such as lively, brightly coloured, buzzing with activity? Although all of these may be considered positive attributes, denoting a busy and cheerful learning environment, for the child with ASD they may represent over-stimulation and prompt a need to escape. And when you closed your eyes, were you very aware of chairs scraping on the floor, or the lights buzzing, or noises from outside? Did it feel unpleasant in any way? Which of these factors could be changed to reduce over-stimulation for children with ASD, without reducing the attractiveness of the room as a learning environment?

_____

_____

_____

_____

Although you are not in sole charge of the classroom, try to be more aware of the physical environment in which you work, and the possible aspects of that environment which may not be helpful to children with ASD.

Sean finds it so hard to concentrate in class he has to resort to putting his fingers in his ears. Although this successfully blocks out the sounds of the classroom, it means that he doesn't hear what the teacher says either.

An adult with Asperger's declares that he cannot look at a colleague who is wearing bold stripes or bright reds, oranges or hot pinks.

Here are some *Don'ts* relating to impairment in imagination:

- Don't expect children with ASD to be socially motivated – i.e. doing something to please the teacher or because everyone else is doing it.
- Don't expect children with ASD to relay messages to parents. Remember, if they know something, they assume that everyone else knows it too. So you need to tell Mum or Dad about the parents evening or the school trip.
- Don't overreact when the child takes you literally. If you use the phrase 'you need to pull your socks up' children with ASD are likely to do that – whether you mean it literally or metaphorically. Remember to be more careful of the way you express yourself.
- Don't expect a lengthy attention span – the child with ASD is easily distracted (by inner thoughts or external stimuli).

 A teacher recalls a child with ASD who refused to come into the main part of the classroom, preferring to sit near the door next to the coats and bags. She considered a variety of reasons for this, and eventually realized that the classroom walls were painted different colours – a bright white for most of the room but a muddy brown in the areas near the coats.

Sensory integration

Dr Jean Ayres, who founded the Ayres Clinic in the USA in 1976, was an occupational therapist (OT) and licensed clinical psychologist. In her work as an OT, Jean Ayres was interested in the way in which sensory processing and motor planning disorders interfere with daily life function and learning. She used the phrase *sensory integration* to describe how each of our senses works with the others to give a complete picture to our brain of who we are physically, where we are, and what is going on around us. We filter the world through our senses. For most children, effective sensory integration occurs automatically and develops during ordinary childhood activities. As babies play with their toes or reach for mobiles they are taking in information through their senses, processing and integrating it within the central nervous system, then using the information to plan and organize behaviour. Neural pathways are built that make future decisions and actions possible. Here is a useful way to think about the process.

Imagine an intrepid explorer wanting to cross a steep ravine where there is no bridge. Luckily there is a single strong rope going from one side to the other. He crosses safely using his hands and feet. It is an incredibly strenuous process. The next time he needs to cross he finds that there are two ropes. Now he crosses by walking across the lower rope and balancing hand over hand on the upper rope. The next time he needs to cross he uses a little chair suspended beneath the ropes to ferry himself across. At last a bridge is built across the chasm and he walks across easily and with certainty.

So it is for us. Early sensory integration provides a crucial foundation for later, more complex learning and behaviour. For some children, however, the process takes effort and attention, and may never be totally efficient. Problems in learning, development, or behaviour occur when there is a dysfunction in the process of sensory integration. For example, infants who have issues with touch will struggle with tactile tasks as basic as feeding.

'Sensory integration is the organization of sensation for use.'
Jean Ayres

In addition to the usual five senses – olfactory (smell), tactile (touch), auditory (hearing), visual (seeing), gustatory (taste) – we need to be aware of two other senses: vestibular (balance and movement) and the proprioceptive (awareness of where you are in space – we know what our body is doing without looking).

Jean Ayres considered severe difficulty with sensory processing and integration to be a 'hallmark' of ASD. She identified the following signs of Sensory Integrative Dysfunction:

- overly sensitive to touch (known as tactile defensive), movement, sights, or sounds
- under-reactive to touch, movement, sights, or sounds
- easily distracted
- social and/or emotional problems
- activity level that is unusually high or unusually low
- physical clumsiness or apparent carelessness
- impulsive, lacking in self control
- difficulty making transitions from one situation to another
- inability to unwind or calm self
- poor self-concept
- delays in speech, language or motor skills
- delays in academic achievement.

Activity

Which of these categories do your children with ASD fit into?

_____

_____

_____

_____

If you have any experience of children with ASD you will have noticed that they may seek out certain sensations (for example, spinning or hand-flapping). They may also avoid or try to reduce the impact of other sensations (noise, for example) by screaming or self-harming. Endorphins are released from the pituitary gland during times of pain or stress. Known as 'natural painkillers', they block pain impulses carried to the brain, reducing pain and stress. Self-harming appears to induce endorphin release. Self-harming, rocking or screaming soften the impact and discomfort caused by environmental stimuli. Children who have difficulties processing sensation also have difficulties producing appropriate responses. As a result, children who are merely jostled may retaliate by hitting out because they are unable to interpret the sensation accurately.

Can anything be done to enable children with ASD to process information from their sense more efficiently and so increase engagement and learning and, almost inevitably, reduce inappropriate behaviour patterns such as flapping, biting or sniffing others? Fortunately, the answer is Yes. The first step is to have an assessment from an occupational thera-pist, the professional who deals with Sensory Integrative Dysfunction. The assessment usually consists of standardized testing and structured observations, and results in a programme of activities to provide sensory experiences most helpful to that child at that point in their development.

Joe has a whole collection of fleece jackets and is rarely seen without one, even on very hot days. When complimented on his smartness in a suit on a special occasion he said, as if talking about a friend, 'I miss my fleece'. Something about the weight and texture of a fleece jacket provides Joe with a sensory experience he needs.

As more and more information is relayed through our senses to the brain we become more efficient at adapting to our environment and using our bodies more expertly.

- Exploring food and everything else with hands, fingers and mouth is all part of the information-gathering, as is throwing toys, shouting, being bounced on Grandpa's knee, cuddled by Mum and thrown up in the air by Dad.
- We adults feed information to children's senses as we play 'peep-bo' or build towers for them to knock down.
- Important vestibular (balancing) senses are developed as we push children on swings and later as they walk on walls and play on rope bridges.
- Climbing, jumping and skipping aid proprioceptive development – the understanding of themselves in relation to space and to things around them. It is our proprioceptive sense that enables us to reach out just as far as we need to close a door with just enough force.
- Pre-writing skills are developed as we allow children to play with water, sand, mud, jelly, chocolate pudding, etc.

You will have noticed differing levels in these skills among your general school population. Some children are much better at throwing and catching than others. Some are better at climbing or running. Some find manipulating small objects easier than others. Some form letters and numbers with ease, others do not. This is also true of adults. With practice we could improve any of our skills, but typically if we are 'naturally good' at running we tend to like running, are motivated to run and so we automatically improve our running, making the gap wider between ourselves and those not 'naturally good' at running. The same principle applies to other skills such as physical, musical and mathematical.

The inefficient neurological processing of information through the senses is known as Sensory Integrative Dysfunction. Children with ASD have difficulties with processing information through their senses resulting in hypersensitivity (called sensory overload) or hypo-sensitivity (*hypo* meaning low). This causes problems with both learning and behaviour. Children with ASD may be hypersensitive to noise (for example) but hypo-sensitive to touch.

Tell-tale signs
Children who are hypersensitive to sound may:

- put their hands over their ears
- dislike certain sounds and pitches
- fear loud noises
- hum or scream to block out noises.

Children who are hyposensitive to sound may:

- show no reaction or aversion to loud sounds
- enjoy loud rhythmic noises
- create sounds to stimulate hearing
- hold noisy toys close to their ear.

Children who are hypersensitive to touch may:

- hate being touched or hugged
- hate hair-washing and nail-cutting
- refuse to wear certain clothes
- take off clothes/shoes
- hate messy activities.

Children who are hyposensitive to touch may:

- self-harm
- ignore cuts/bruises
- seem not to feel pain
- want rough and tumble
- like tight clothes.

Children who are visually hypersensitive may:

- dislike eye contact
- glance at things quickly
- use peripheral vision
- dislike bright/fluorescent/flashing lights
- be fascinated by small objects/examine them in detail.

Children who are visually hyposensitive may:

- look intently at lights
- touch everything in unfamiliar surroundings
- move finger/objects in front of eyes
- be distressed by changes of lighting from one room to another.

Some children have gustatory (eating) sensitivities and may:

- gag or regurgitate
- eat everything, including soil and faeces
- eat a limited range of foods.

Some children have olfactory (smell) sensitivities and may:

- sniff or lick people and/or things
- dislike strong smells
- want to wear the same clothes day after day.

Designing individual programmes to help children with ASD cope with Sensory Integrative Dysfunction is a role for occupational therapists. They will suggest ways of calming (for hypersensitivities) or alerting (for hyposensitivities). They may suggest 'sensory snacks' to help lessen the effects of certain sensory stimuli. These have nothing to do with eating, but refer to small amounts of 'therapy' throughout the day to reduce sensitivities generally. Part of your role is to remember that controlling sensory issues can affect behaviour and learning and make for happier children.

TEACCH (Treatment and Education of Autistic and Related Communication-Handicapped Children)

In this next section we will look in some detail at the TEACCH programme, because it addresses all three areas of the triad and can be used extensively for children with ASD.

TEACCH was developed in the early 1970s by Eric Schopler and his colleagues in North Carolina, USA, as a training and research programme for children and adults with ASD, whatever their ages or intellectual ability. It is a highly structured, visual system, which enables children and adults with ASD to make sense of their day, and work more independently. As we have already discussed in Chapter 2, children with ASD have an intense need for predictability, structure and sameness. They need and enjoy routines, although they are unable to set them up themselves. They are also, for the most part, visual learners – they process information better when they see it – but there are no such things as 'unimportant details' for children with ASD. So they need others to pick out the relevant details for them. TEACCH satisfies all of these needs by providing a visual schedule for each child. Some people refer to them as timelines or timetables. Whichever term you choose, consistency is important, and the way you present information on the schedule must match the level of understanding of the child. Imagine a hierarchy of visual communication with abstract symbols (such as words) at the higher end, and concrete objects (actual toys or clothes) at the lower end. A photograph of the object is the next step up from the object itself, followed by a drawing of the object, then words alone. Schedules must be presented in a format the children understand – even at their most stressed!

Hierarchy of Visual Communication

TEACCH can be used in a variety of ways and formats.

Visual schedules – outlining a sequence of events or activities

In a class of primary-aged children with severe learning difficulties and ASD, each child has his/her own schedule or timeline on the wall (see illustrations overleaf). Each has a different coloured background and a photo of the child at the top with his or her name. The timelines are laminated and pinned firmly to the wall. Each timeline is separated into 4 sections by a thick black marker line, and each section has a small piece of Velcro attached to it. Laminated photographs of activities, people or locations around school have been taken with a digital camera, copied many times, laminated and filed (a time-consuming but essential task). Before the children come into class each day the first four activities of the day will already be in place – typically, a photo of assembly, followed by a photo of the register, followed by a photo representing the first session (e.g. the story bag we are using) followed by a photo of drinks and snacks. Schedules may run vertically or horizontally. The children have learned to go up to their timeline when called, and respond verbally (or by signing) in response to the prompt: 'Time for . . .' They take the next photo on the timeline and go the area designated for that activity. At the conclusion of the activity each child returns, puts their photo in the 'finished' box beneath the timeline and takes the next photo. During break, new photos are put in place to indicate the activities leading up to lunchtime.

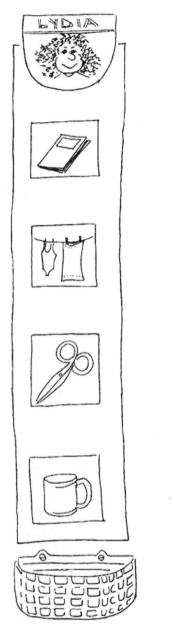

Visual Schedules

This visual schedule is very effective for children with ASD. It is consistent and predictable, it reduces anxiety about the events of the day and it clearly indicates and reminds children what will happen next, so preparing them for transition. Visual timelines also facilitate greater independence.

The prompts on the visual schedule depend on the individual child's level of understanding. Some children need concrete objects such as swimming towels or paint brushes to inform them about their activities; some can work with photographs or pictures; others can manage words. In all cases, it is the visual structure that is important. It is worth remembering too that for some children words may be meaningful only on a good day. Schedules need to use communication that is effective, no matter what is happening. Often in times of great anxiety, it is the schedule alone that gives stability and moves a child along.

Gary Mesibov and Victoria Shea of the TEACCH programme argue that ASD can be seen as a culture with its own ways of communicating and seeing the world. They see the aim of the TEACCH programme as enabling children with ASD to fit into society by respecting their strengths and by giving them the skills they need – not by trying to make them 'normal'.

Activity

Stop and think for a moment of the classroom where you work. We talked in Chapter 2 about the routines of schools and classrooms. How many of those routines could be represented as a series of pictures? We have already referred to the timetable for the day, but can you think of any other series of actions which could be represented using a TEACCH-type format?

_____

_____

_____

_____

_____

Visual sequences – strings of instructions or information

Here are some examples of visual sequences for areas of the classroom or times of the day that can be illustrated using the principles of TEACCH:

- visual timelines next to the washbasin, giving step-by-step instructions for hand washing and drying
- visual timelines after swimming sessions enabling children with ASD to dress independently
- visual 'lists' enabling a child to complete a series of tasks around the class or school
- visual shopping lists to guide children around a shop, helping them choose and pay for goods independently
- visual lists indicating equipment or books needed for the day.

More able children can be helped to make their own visual sequences, reminding them of sets of instructions, or a series of actions or activities which they need to follow.

Visual parameters – defining the limits of an activity

Children with ASD have difficulty gauging when an activity will end – or if it will go on forever. We can relate to that, can't we? How many of us would like to start a day's work – or even a particular task – not knowing when (or if) it would finish? To overcome this potential difficulty, TEACCH recommends 'shoebox' activities.

Activities which have been planned for the child are literally kept in shoeboxes (or a similar size container). The child quickly learns that the activity consists of only those things contained in the one box – for example: only ten pegs to fit into holes and then the dexterity task is finished; or only eight shapes and then the sorting task is finished; or only twenty pairs of objects or cards and then matching task is finished. The concept of 'finished' is important. The visual and obvious extent of the activity reduces stress for children with ASD.

TEACCH principles can also be used for another aspect of these activities, particularly for children with learning difficulties. Each child has his or her own workstation, and at the child's eye level (when he is seated) is a visual timeline, which is laminated and firmly attached to the wall. A horizontal Velcro strip has been stuck to the timeline, and attached to the Velcro are three separate (laminated) shapes, each of a different colour. A matching coloured shape is attached to each activity box on the table alongside the workstation. Working from left to right the child takes a shape and matches it to the shape on a box, pulls the box onto the table in front of him and completes the task inside. The finished box is then put on the floor. The child matches the next shape on the timeline to the relevant box and completes that activity, and so on. If the activities in the boxes are those the child can complete without help, the whole procedure also helps to develop the skills of following a timeline and working independently.

Shoebox tasks

Stop and think about children you work with – what sorts of activities could be used as 'shoebox' tasks for them?

_____

_____

_____

_____

_____

TEACCH provides visual structure and so gives children with ASD the skills they need to function in school or in society by making use of their strengths. Children with ASD work well when there is structure and routine, and when expectations are clear.

There are critics of allowing children with ASD to work alone at a workstation because it does not help them develop social skills. However, Clare Sainsbury reports from personal experience that working collaboratively in groups can be painful and ineffective for children with ASD. The decision as to when children work alone and when they work collaboratively should be made on the same basis for children with ASD as it is for neurotypical children: the objective of each session is always the main consideration. All children sometimes need quiet time to work on a particular task. At others times, working in pairs or small groups, they can develop social skills in addition to working on a task. And in each case there is the delicate balance of the child's needs and abilities. When we are out of our comfort zones how difficult it is to function effectively, let alone feel calm and happy in our work?

Other teaching theories and strategies

Brain Gym™

Brain Gym™ is a movement-based programme used to integrate the brain, senses and body in order to enhance learning. It can also be used to improve attention and behaviour. Founded in the USA by Dr Paul Dennison, it is now recognized and used in many countries as an educational tool. It was first created to help children and adults with learning difficulties such as dyslexia, dyspraxia and ADHD (Attention Deficit Hyperactivity Disorder). The main theory behind Brain Gym™ is that physical movement or exercise stimulates and helps brain functioning in:

- academic skills – reading, writing, spelling and maths
- memory and concentration
- balance and physical co-ordination
- communication and language skills.

These are obviously areas that are important for all children, but particularly helpful for children with ASD. In the UK, Brain Gym™ programmes are offered through the Educational Kinesiology Foundation (further details can be found on their website – www.braingym.org.uk).

Higashi

Higashi is another exercise-based approach, and is based on Daily Life Therapy, which was developed by Dr Kiyo Kitahara in Japan. It is a holistic approach which aims to bring all aspects of the child into harmony. The goal is for children's development to come as close as possible to 'normal' – physically, emotionally and intellectually – and for children to achieve social independence and dignity. There is a significant emphasis on physical education and vigorous exercise to reduce anxiety, increase stamina and coordination, and develop group interactions. Higashi is typically not used in ordinary schools to any great extent. It is more often found in privately run Higashi schools.

Lovaas

The Lovaas method is based on the work of American psychologist, Ivar Lovaas. It is a very intensive behaviour therapy approach for children with ASD and other disorders. Dr Lovaas worked with institutionalized, non-verbal children who had been diagnosed as autistic, trying to develop their verbal communication using applied behavioural analysis. One of the major problems he encountered was that most of the children lost their verbal skills when the treatment programme stopped and they returned to the institution. However, those who returned home at the end of the treatment retained some skills, especially if their parents took an interest in the programme. This led Lovaas to change the setting of the treatment, and he began to work with younger children in their own homes with the help of the parents. In 1987 Lovaas published the results of his work and showed for the first time that behavioural strategies could apparently counteract some of the impairments associated with ASD. He claimed that almost half of the children in his home-based programme were functioning normally by age seven, while another large proportion (40 per cent) still showed characteristics of ASD but had made substantial progress. Only about one child in ten seemed to receive no benefit. A follow-up study in 1993 showed that most of the children still appeared to be functioning normally into their teens.

The recommended Lovaas treatment ideally begins before a child is three and-a-half, is home-based, and consists of 40 hours a week of intensive one-to-one therapy – six to eight hours a day, five to seven days a week, for two or more years. Because the therapy is so intensive it needs a team of at least three people, all of whom must be properly trained. Family participation is very important. Each of the skills which the child needs to learn are broken down into small, easily achieveable tasks that are taught in a very structured way with lots of praise and other rewards. As the child progresses the treatment can be split between home and school. The Lovaas treatment is long and intensive, which means it can also be very expensive. It is also obviously not a programme that a teacher can just decide to start up for a child with ASD in the class. Typically the parents will opt for Lovaas treatment. The NAS website has contact information for Lovaas programmes in the UK (see the Appendix for details).

Chapter summary

In this chapter we have considered some of the strategies that can be used to help children with ASD to function more effectively, emphasizing the strengths of their condition rather than the difficulties. If children with ASD are to function in families or take part in a range of activities in school, they have to learn to tolerate the world around them with all its sounds, colours and smells. However, tolerance should and usually can be built up slowly. Interestingly Hans Asperger's recommended approach to effective teaching was to give 'true understanding and genuine affection'.

Activity

Reflective Journal

What have I learned in this chapter?

Looking back on what you have read in the chapter, and the suggested Do's and Don'ts, which approaches do you feel would be appropriate for the children you work with? List three Do's here that you could easily incorporate into your current role.

1. _____

_____

2. _____

_____

3. _____

_____

Now list three Don'ts that you could eradicate from your work.

1. _____

_____

2. _____

_____

3. _____

_____

Remember: Before implementing any new strategies you must consult with your supervising teacher(s).

Conclusions

At the beginning of this book, we told you that it was written specifically for people like yourself who wish to increase their understanding of ASD and of the children it affects. While it is true that your work in the classroom must always be carried out under the supervision of qualified professionals, it is also true that increasing your knowledge and understanding of children and how they learn is important and useful. Some of what you have learned about ASD will help you in your work with all children. We will discuss this later. First let's review what we have covered in this book.

In Chapter 1 we gave you an overview of ASD and how our understanding of it has developed historically through the work and writings of researchers and practitioners, as well as parents and carers. We also looked at myths surrounding ASD – myths relating to the causes and the characteristics of ASD – all of which muddy our understanding unless they are dispelled. ASD is not always easy to diagnose and can be confused with other conditions. It is often found alongside other conditions. It is not a particularly common disorder but it is a lifelong and pervasive condition for which there is no cure. TAs working in mainstream schools are most likely to encounter children with Asperger syndrome. TAs in special schools probably work with children who have classic or Kanner's autism. Some TAs work with children who have not been diagnosed with ASD but who show autistic-type behaviours alongside other special educational needs.

Activity

Think back to Chapter 1. What struck you most forcibly when you read it?

_____

_____

_____

_____

Take a moment to record some misconceptions, or myths, about ASD that you can now dismiss.

_____

_____

_____

_____

In Chapter 2 we looked at some of the common difficulties experienced by children with ASD – the effects it has on their lives and behaviour. We referred to what Lorna Wing and Judith Gould termed the Triad of Impairment – that is, significant difficulties, or impairments, in all the three areas of:

- communication
- social development and interaction
- imagination, or flexibility of thinking.

Many children with ASD have no verbal language. Children with Asperger's often have no obvious difficulties with expressive language (speech). However, their understanding of the nuances and subtleties of receptive language is impaired, often resulting in misunderstandings. In this chapter we considered how these impairments impact on relationships and on the ability to empathize. We also discussed the typical hyper- and hyposensitivities associated with ASD, as well as obsessive and bizarre behaviours often demonstrated by these children. Finally, we considered coping skills for the child and for their family.

Activity

Think about the information given in Chapter 2 and how it affected your thinking about ASD. What one thing did you change in your attitude or practice as a TA because of what you read? Make a note of it here.

_____

_____

_____

_____

_____

Now take a moment to consider what the chapter confirmed for you, in terms of your beliefs and knowledge of ASD.

_____

_____

_____

_____

_____

_____

In Chapter 3 we looked at some general principles of behaviour management. We considered the ABCs of behaviour and learned that all behaviours have antecedents and consequences. If we want to affect children's behaviour, we need to look at the antecedents and consequences, to see what can be changed. In this way we manage behaviour. Effective behaviour management consists of setting up a classroom environment where appropriate and positive behaviours are promoted and encouraged, and where negative and distractive behaviour is minimized. In this chapter we considered the behaviours that are linked to or result from the Triad of Impairment. We asked the question: can children with ASD control their behaviour? We concluded that with proper support they can be helped to behave in ways that are socially acceptable, less harmful to themselves or others and more conducive to academic learning and social progress. ASD has been described as a condition of almost permanent stress. As a TA working with children with ASD, you are in a good position to reduce some of that stress. As you apply your understanding of those classroom factors which may cause distress or discomfort, you can remove or minimize these negative influences and so facilitate learning and a sense of well-being.

Activity

Think back to Chapter 3 and the principles of behaviour management we discussed. Select two things you can start doing today to use a more positive approach to behaviour management.

1. _____

    _____

2. _____

    _____

In Chapter 4 we considered the best approaches to use when teaching children with ASD. We looked at ways in which you can build on the strengths of ASD.

We concluded that:

■ Visual prompts and graphics aid the development of communication skills and reduce the anxiety (and potential challenging behaviour) caused by uncertainty about forthcoming events and dislike of change.

■ Various strategies aid the development of social interaction; we emphasized the importance of safe places for appropriate relaxation activities, the teaching of social behaviours, and the explaining of social situations.

■ Classroom organization and the physical environment, including the structure and routines of the day help develop flexibility in thinking and behaviour.

We outlined the PECS and TEACCH programmes in addition to other teaching approaches, such as Brain Gym™ and Lovaas, all of which have been shown to benefit children with ASD to a greater or lesser extent. At the end of Chapter 4 you were asked to consider how much of this is your responsibility as a TA, bearing in mind that you work under the direction of a supervising professional.

Activity

Think back to Chapter 4. Which strategies do you feel you could incorporate into your daily work in order to provide more effective support for children with ASD? Take a moment to list two here.

1. _____

_____

2. _____

_____

General principles

We would like you to remember three important general principles when working with children with ASD.

1. Show tolerance and empathy for the children.

Now that you have a better understanding of what life can be like for children with ASD with all its anxieties, you should be able to make the necessary allowances and to adapt the way you work to better suit their needs. Remember what we discussed in Chapter 3: we change children's behaviour by changing the antecedents and/or the consequences. In some situations that may mean changing our own behaviour first.

2. Provide support for parents and families.

Typically, most interactions between school and family occur via the teacher. And this is how it should be. However, with the approval of your supervising teacher, you can provide useful support to parents of children with ASD by:

- Offering to make TEACCH-type timelines for children to use at home. Ask parents to provide appropriate photographs. But don't be surprised if they do not take up your offer. This may be one more thing that they haven't the energy to deal with and they may not see the usefulness of the timeline being worth the effort it would take to get things organized.

- Being accommodating if children come into school with hair uncombed, wearing pyjamas with their school-clothes in a bag. The smallest upset that morning may have made dressing and washing impossible. Getting children to school on time and in good order can be difficult enough under any circumstances. So be kind and give parents the benefit of the doubt. Just do what you can to make up the difference.

- Listening if parents complain about the child being a pain. Let them complain. Don't hold it against them. They are probably just having a bad day. Just acknowledge the difficulties without trying to provide solutions. They do love their child, but life is hard and unrelenting for them and not necessarily full of support. At school you work as a team, and you go home, and still some days seem hard. You may be the only person they feel will understand. That is why they complain to you. They do not expect you to have the answer so don't try and give one – just listen.

Bear in mind that many of the principles we have discussed – particularly those in Chapter 4 – can be used with all children, not just those with ASD. This is because they are general principles which facilitate effective communication, social interaction and flexibility of thought.

You will communicate more effectively with most children by:

- Simplifying your language, particularly if you notice that a child does not seem able to respond – better to start simply and work up to more complex language rather than start at a level which is too difficult, when you risk confusing a child and lowering his or her confidence and self-esteem.

- Giving only one or two instructions at a time rather than a long string.

- giving children time to process your question as well as formulating their answer.

You will enhance social interactions and broaden all children's social skills by:

- Allowing children time to work alone as well as giving them opportunities to work in pairs or groups.

- Explaining the rules governing social interactions and collaborative work – not all children come to school with these types of norms, whether they have ASD or not; this is particularly true for children of other cultures.

- Ensuring that all of the children you work with treat each other with respect, no matter what their differences. You can set the example yourself by showing your appreciation of the diverse attributes and differing strengths of your pupils.

- Indicating that bullying is never acceptable.

You will assist all children to develop flexibility if you:

- Provide routines and predictability in the course of the day.

- Allow them to have their own systems and preferences, provided they do not interfere with the general running of the classroom.

- Prepare them in advance for a change in activity by telling them they will have to put the toys/book/computer away in [tell them how many] minutes. Sometimes it is helpful to use a kitchen timer.

The impairments associated with ASD can never be solved. Often it takes time, and of course patience, to gain the trust of children with ASD and enable them to feel more in control of their environment. You can enhance the learning environment and school experience for all children (including those with ASD) by being willing to learn about their strengths and weaknesses and then using the principles we have mentioned. The truth is that we often do not know how children think. We assume that we know. Most children manage well enough in school – they follow instructions and do what they are asked and they appear to be learning to a greater or lesser degree. As long as all that is happening, we often look no further.

How will this change what I do as a TA?

As always when we acquire new information, we ask ourselves the question: What difference does this make? Or, what difference should it make to what I do from now on? This really is your decision, and it depends on why you picked up this book in the first place. Were you just curious, having heard the terms 'autism' and 'Autistic Spectrum Disorders' and wondered what they really meant? Do you perhaps have a vested interest in the subject because you work with or know a child with ASD? Whichever is the case, we hope that what you have read will influence you in a positive way, and will lead to improvements in the lives of children with ASD through your increased understanding.

Without a doubt, ASD is an enigma – largely because it is unpredictable and so very varied. Any one individual with ASD may surprise us by their reactions and behaviour in different situations and with the passing of time. But it is an enigma that we are at least beginning to understand in terms of its enormity for those who are on the spectrum – its pervasive nature, which affects every aspect of their lives, and its permanence as a lifetime condition.

Appendix

Recommended reading

The following is a selection of books relating to ASD from a variety of perspectives, all of which we would recommend as being very readable and informative. There are many more good books on ASD, which you can find through a search in your local library catalogue or on the internet. You will also find more books about ASD listed on the Continuum website (www.continuumbooks.com), including:

- Sarah Worth's *Autistic Spectrum Disorder*
- Diana Seach's *Supporting Children with Autism in Mainstream Schools*
- Jill Morgan's *The Teaching Assistant's Guide to Managing Behaviour*

Tony Attwood is an Australian university professor who takes the perspective that people with Asperger's think differently, not defectively. His book is *The Complete Guide to Asperger Syndrome* (published in 2006 by Jessica Kingsley).

Uta Frith's *Autism: Explaining the Enigma* was first published in 1989 but is now in its second, revised edition (published by Blackwell in 2003).

Temple Grandin wrote *Thinking in Pictures* from her personal perspective as an adult with ASD. An American university professor, she designs mechanisms for humane handling of cattle (published by Bloomsbury Publishing in 2006).

Mark Haddon's book *The Curious Incident of the Dog in the Night-Time* is written as a novel, but has won acclaim for how well it portrays the thinking of a teenager with ASD (published by Vintage in 2004).

Kathy Hoopman's book *All Cats have Asperger Syndrome* is a clever illustration of the characteristics of ASD, in words and pictures. When 14-year-old Joe, who has Asperger's, read it he said. 'That's me. That's what its like', and the rest of his family could only agree (published in 2006 by Jessica Kingsley).

Luke Jackson wrote *Freaks, Geeks & Asperger Syndrome: A User's Guide to Adolescence* when he was himself a teenager (published in 2002 by Jessica Kingsley).

Charlotte Moore's book *George & Sam* describes life with her three sons – two of whom have ASD – and the many different strategies and treatments which she used to support their learning and understanding (published in 2004 by Penguin).

Clare Sainsbury's *Martian in the Playground* describes what school can be like for children with ASD. Based on her own experience and interviews with other adults with ASD in several countries, it paints a fascinating but rather discouraging picture of how poorly ASD is understood, and the effects that has on the child (published in 2002 by Lucky Duck Publishing).

Daniel Tammet, an autistic savant for whom colour defines numbers, wrote *Born on a Blue Day* to describe his life with ASD (publisher by Hodder Paperback in 2007).

Lorna Wing's *The Autistic Spectrum: A Guide for Parents and Professionals* was first published in 1996. It has continued to be a popular and there is an updated edition (published by Constable in 2003).

No set of recommendations for information on ASD would be complete without mention of Ros Blackburn, who has 'appeared' in several places already in this book. However, to our knowledge Ros has never written a book, nor does she have a website. You will find many references to her if you conduct an internet search, but there is no substitute for hearing her speak – which she does so eloquently – and often at the invitation of local support groups for ASD.

Organizations and websites

The following is a selection of organizations and websites relating to ASD. They are all UK-based organizations. An internet search using the keywords ASD or autism will provide you with a list of many more sites, worldwide. There is now a great deal of information about ASD out there!

National Autistic Society (NAS) www.nas.org.uk
The NAS offers a wide variety of services to individuals with autism and their families. This includes social programmes, conferences, an Advocacy for Education service, a helpline, and a quarterly magazine, *Communication*. The NAS website contains a huge amount of useful and interesting information as well as links to other related sites. There are also details of the 'Make School Make Sense' campaign to improve the school experience for children with ASD, with a Teachers' Awareness Pack that you can read or download.

The Department for Education and Science (DfES) Teacher-Net website www.teachernet.gov.uk
This website contains several documents and sources of information relating to ASD, including:

- The *Need-to-know Guide: Autism.*
- The Teachers online magazine, which you can search for different topics of interest – for instance, the July 2004 issue has two articles on autism.
- *Autistic Spectrum Disorders: Good Practice Guidance*, 2002 – look for this under the Special Educational Needs section.

The Autism Research Unit (ARU) at the University of Sunderland
www.osiris.sunderland.ac.uk/autism/
This website has general information, as well as details of conferences and research relating to ASD, and links to other useful sites.

The Autism Research Centre (ARC) at the University of Cambridge www.autismresearchcentre.com/arc
Directed by Dr Simon Baron-Cohen, the ARC has a number of different research projects related to ASD, as well as the CLASS project for adults with ASD who may never have been previously diagnosed. From this site you can even volunteer to take part in a variety of research projects relating to ASD.

Autism Independent UK (formerly the Society for the Autistically Handicapped – SFTAH) **www.autismuk.com**
Autism Independent UK is a non-medical advice and information centre. It also offers training in using the TEACCH programme and social stories.

Glossary

Asperger Syndrome
A form of high-functioning autism, named after Dr Hans Asperger, an Austrian doctor whose research was first published in German in the 1940s, and described a condition he called autistic pathology.

Autism
A general term for what is now referred to as Autistic Spectrum Disorders (ASD). The word autism comes from the Greek word *autos* (meaning self) because of the inner focus of children with ASD.

Autist
A term sometimes used for a person with ASD.

Autistic Spectrum Disorders
The more recent term for autism, recognizing the wide range and variety of behaviours and manifestations of autism.

Disability versus inability
A disability is a recognized impairment which limits effective functioning and the so-called normal activities of daily living. This may be caused by an inability in one or more areas. However not all inabilities limit life functioning, so they would not all be considered disabilities. An inability to play the piano, for example, would not be particularly limiting, whereas an inability to communicate obviously would.

Echolalia
Repeating or echoing what someone else has said. Echolalia is common in classic or low-functioning autism.

Hypersensitivity
Over-sensitivity to sensory input (touch, smell, sounds, colours, etc.), producing a tendency to be either fearful or very cautious.

Hyposensitivity
Under-sensitivity to sensory stimuli (heat/cold, etc.) leading to a tendency to crave intense sensations, or to withdraw and be difficult to engage.

Individual Education Plan (IEP)
A working document stating short- or medium-term educational objectives. It is monitored regularly.

Impairment versus lack
An impairment is a partial inability in a particular area, but can vary considerably between individuals. As an example, visual impairments may range from needing reading glasses to almost total blindness. However the word does not suggest a complete lack in that area. Thus children with ASD who have impairments in communication, social interactions and imagination rarely have a total lack of skill in these areas, even if the impairment is severe.

Kanner, Leo
American psychiatrist who first identified the characteristics of what he termed 'early infantile autism,' as his patients were all children. What is now known as Kanner's or classic autism is not confined to children, but does always have associated learning difficulties.

Occupational Therapist (OT)
A professional whose training in sensory integration enables him or her to assess children and design individualized programmes which can be carried out on a daily basis in the classroom or at home.

Profound and Multiple Learning Difficulties (PMLD)
A categorization of pupils who have more than one serious difficulty affecting their learning. Typically these pupils are placed in special schools.

Prosody
Intonation, or a varied tone of voice and emphasis, that give speech interesting rhythm and sound patterns, rather than the flat, monotone patterns of speech typical of children with ASD.

Savant
A person who has extreme ability in a specific area, such as the ability to calculate numbers instantaneously. Although this is often associated with ASD, not more than one in ten of people with ASD have these extreme abilities.

Sensory diet
The multi-sensory experiences a person naturally seeks on a daily basis to satisfy sensory appetite. Children with ASD will not naturally be able to provide this for themselves, but an occupational therapist can plan and provide sensory 'meals' or 'snacks' to help regulate a child with sensory impairment or dysfunction.

Sensory integration
The neurological process of taking in information through the senses from one's own body and from the environment, organizing and unifying this information and using it to plan and execute adaptive responses to different challenges. For

example, if – as we step out of the front door – we feel that the air is cool and see that it is raining, we go back and put on a coat before leaving the house. Dysfunction in sensory integration is the inefficient neurological processing of information through the senses, causing problems with learning and behaviour.

Self-harm

Common among children with ASD, the pain created by self-harming is known to produce endorphins which provide comfort and stress release. Self-harming also helps to block out stimuli (noises or other sensory input) which children find uncomfortable or disturbing.

Severe Learning Difficulties (SLD)

A categorization of pupils whose difficulties are severe (rather than moderate or specific) and affect their learning.

Spectrum

Another word for a range or scale of intensity. In the case of Autistic Spectrum Disorders it represents the range of abilities and varying levels of intensity of the characteristics and behaviours that are typical of autism.